WOMEN IN THE CHURCH

WOMEN IN THE CHURCH

a pastoral approach

Derek Prime

CROSSWAY BOOKS

All scripture quotations are from the New
International Version. Copyright © 1973, 1978, 1984
International Bible Society. Published by Hodder
and Stoughton.

ISBN: 1–85684–042–5

Printed in Great Britain for Crossway Books,
Kingfisher House, 7 High Green, Great Shelford,
Cambridge CB2 1SG by Cox & Wyman Ltd, Reading.
Typeset by Avocet Typesetters, Ltd, Bicester, Oxon.

Contents

Introduction

Why another book on women's ministry? That is not an unreasonable question since we are in danger of being swamped by literature on the subject.

The seemingly logical development of the arguments of contemporary feminism makes women's ordination the principal concern for some. For others the issue is the proper exercise of spiritual gifts within the body of Christ. For not a few it is simply a matter of human progress. They argue that as earlier this century horror was expressed at the thought of women doctors and drivers, so the similar horror some express at the thought of women ministers will soon prove itself just as old-fashioned. Approaches to the subject are numerous, as is the range of influences behind any consideration of it.

My motive for trying to contribute to the present discussion is pastoral. I want, if I can, to argue for an approach that unites God's people rather than divides them, believing that in the end openness to the Scriptures and the Holy Spirit must lead clearly in that direction.

The most important issue is the authority of Scripture. Are the Scriptures authoritative in *all* matters of faith and practice? That question cannot be shirked, and we must try to answer it.

At the same time, most of us who have exercised leadership in the Church in the past must confess that men's ministry has been stressed to the neglect of women's. Women's gifts have been, and are, frequently neglected. Some women feel insecure, devastated and robbed of their ministry. Where such feelings are justified, that situation needs to be remedied. Those of us who hold most firmly to the authority of Scripture need to admit that we have sometimes been conditioned all too easily by traditions rather than by the testing of our convictions and practices by the principles of Scripture.

Some of us in leadership have often felt that greater attention should be given to women's ministry but, aware of the suspicion that initiating change provokes, we have opted for a quiet life rather than bold action. Questioning traditional attitudes in well-established churches is bound to promote debate and possible disagreement.

As a result of our neglect, sudden changes regarding women's ministry have taken place nevertheless, not because they have been properly discussed but because understandable dissatisfaction has erupted on account of the failure of those in leadership to review and test the status quo by Scripture.

If the most important spiritual issue is the authority of Scripture, the most pressing practical issue is how to introduce right and necessary changes without dividing the body of Christ, both in our local churches and fellowships and in the wider context of our relationships within the whole body of Christ. Change is never easy. It is not only important to know what needs to be changed, but to discern how change is to be put into practice and its proper timing. To divide the body of Christ is sin.

Questions for discussion

1. What prompts our interest in women's ministry?

2. How far do we feel our own church fellowship provides sufficient scope for women to exercise their gifts?

Chapter One

The Authority of Scripture

Our first question must be, 'What does the Bible teach?' Basic to all Christian faith and practice is God's revelation of himself and of his will. The truths of Christianity are *revealed* truths: they are not the consequence of the human discovery of God but of God's deliberate self-disclosure – a disclosure given uniquely in writing in the Scriptures of the Old and New Testaments, and supremely in the Incarnation of his Son.

Because the Scriptures are God-breathed and God-inspired, they bear their Author's character: they are authoritative, permanent and sufficient. These characteristics are clearly relevant to our subject. In giving rise to the collection of writings that we call the Scriptures or the Bible, God the Holy Spirit anticipated the requirements of God's people throughout the centuries. He ensured that the Scriptures contain all the imperatives (or commands), instructions and principles God's people need, and will need for their guidance.

The special bonus given to God's people at every stage of history is the presence of the Author of the Scriptures, the Holy Spirit, to guide them in their understanding, and to help them to apply the imperatives, instructions and principles of Scripture to personal and corporate life.

This immediately raises important issues. Can we always draw a clear distinction between imperatives, instructions and principles? Should matters of culture influence our interpretation? What if the Holy Spirit's help is not sought? What conclusions are we to draw from the different convictions Christians have upon important subjects like women's ministry?

A distinction can usually be drawn between imperatives, instructions and principles. I say 'usually' because sometimes one may merge into another. The 'golden rule' – that we should love God first and then, second, love our neighbour as ourself – is an imperative, binding upon us at all times. While the application may be a matter of debate on occasions, the obligatory nature of the instruction is not.

Under the heading of imperatives – or commands – there must be included, of course, the Ten Commandments, our Lord's teaching that we should seek first God's kingdom, and his command that we should love one another.

A distinction can often be drawn between instructions and principles, in that an instruction generally comes in the form of a command or a clear direction – for example, our Lord's instructions about baptism and the Communion Service.

Sometimes an instruction and a principle are merged together, and we need to discern the principle behind the initial instruction. This underlines the importance of our appreciating that to apply some biblical instructions and principles properly, we first have to understand the culture of the people to whom they were originally written so that we do not misapply the instructions and principles in our own different culture.

An uncomplicated example is the instruction Peter gives to 'greet one another with a kiss of love' (1 Pet 5:14) – the usual way in which people in the East greeted one another. They did not kiss on the lips as we may do, but upon the cheek, and the custom was not generally exercised between the sexes. J B Phillips appropriately translates this as 'give each other a handshake all round as a sign of love' since this is more in keeping with our own culture, and puts a necessary restraint upon the abuse literal obedience to the command could have in our different manner of kissing. Behind the instruction is the principle that Christians should love one another, and express their love in everyday courtesies as well as in practical help.

Behind practical instructions we often discover the application of fundamental principles of Christian behaviour. The major issue in first-century society of whether or not Christians should eat meat offered to idols seems remote from our circumstances in the West – although certainly not so for some present-day Christians in the East. However, the principles Paul establishes from that situation – especially about behaviour which might cause others to stumble – are precisely what we need for dealing with our totally different morally delicate situations.

Precise instructions concerning all important aspects of church life are not given in the Scriptures, but principles are. The most obvious is church government. The New Testament does not provide a blueprint for how the life of a local church is to be ordered. It does not lay down, for example, how many elders or deacons a church should have, how they should be appointed, and for how long. Sadly, Christians have allowed convictions on these matters to divide them, so that when we affirm ourselves to be Anglican or Presbyterian or Free (ie Independent) churches, we are not making an affirmation about the Christian faith but rather about how we feel a local church's life should be governed.

My personal conviction is that God the Holy Spirit deliberately chose not to provide clear instructions in the New Testament about church order and government. He recognises – as the Church has sometimes failed to do – that circumstances vary so much throughout the world, and even in one country, that different approaches are necessary. Each community of Christians must apply the same principles to its different situations.

When we consider women's ministry in the church, we must make sure, therefore, that we recognise God's *commands* or *imperatives*. We must know what are *instructions* and what are *principles*. We must be prepared to see if either instructions or principles have a different application in the culture of our day than they might have had in the first century. But our

14

conclusions must be based not on human wisdom alone but upon the Scriptures, on account of their final authority. We are not to be guided by contemporary opinion but by what God says.

Tensions and even conflict exist among many groups of Christians today about the exact nature of the Bible's authority, and the degree to which its teaching on subjects such as women's ministry is binding. Some think of the Bible – and the New Testament in particular – as speaking only to the culture of its time with regard to women's ministry, and therefore as not providing a pattern for today's church. Others feel that the Bible simply expresses the religious experience of the first Christians and is not God's revelation for the norms of contemporary conduct.

Much of the debate about women's ministry centres around the apostle Paul's teaching. The suggestion is made that he spoke simply as a man of his day, conditioned by first-century culture. We must consider this more closely when we look later at some of his statements. But we must never forget that Paul wrote with God-given wisdom (2 Pet 3:15), and that his teaching as an apostle was part of the God-given foundation of the Church (Eph 2:20). Paul's constant appeal was to Scripture and not to the practices of Judaism or the accepted standards of the Greek and Roman world. His vital question in any matter of debate was, 'What do the Scriptures say?' He deliberately applied the Scriptures to Apollos and himself, for example, in order to teach the Corinthians to live by Scripture and not to go beyond what was written (1 Cor 4:6). So Paul was already lifting principles first expressed in earlier cultures into a later culture.

Acceptance of the Scriptures' authority is in the final analysis an act of faith. It is not, however, an act of faith contrary to reason. All our personal experience of God has found its source in his revelation in Scripture. It was the Scriptures, as they were preached to us, which gave rise to faith in the Lord Jesus Christ (Rom 10:17). They have subsequently fed us (1 Pet 2:2) and furthered our sanctification (Ps 119:9; Jn 17:17). By meditating upon the Scriptures and obeying them, we know God better and make progress in the Christian life (Ps 1; Jas 1:22–25).

The Scriptures' authority arises from the One who has inspired and given us the Scriptures – God himself. They reveal the truth about his own character and purposes, and also what he values and what he wants his creatures to value. Our Lord Jesus Christ appealed to them as the final authority when important subjects were under discussion (eg Mt 19:4–6).

The Scriptures are specifically called 'the word of Christ' (Col 3:16) and declared to be inspired by 'the Spirit of Christ' (1 Pet 1:11). We cannot separate our Lord Jesus Christ from his Word, just as we cannot separate ourselves from our words. All authority in heaven and on earth has been given to him (Mt 28:18), and he expresses that authority through his Word. He alone is the Head of the Church (Eph 1:22). The manner in which he chooses to govern and guide His church is through his Word, under his Spirit's

16

direction. What the Scriptures say, the Lord Jesus Christ, the Head of the Church, says.

The Scriptures are authoritative, therefore, because they are the Word by which the Lord Jesus Christ rules his people. He intends them to be our guide in all matters of faith and practice. In looking to them for guidance, we look to him. In obeying them, we obey our Lord Jesus Christ and show our love for him (Jn 14:15, 21, 23).

Our Lord Jesus Christ speaks authoritatively to his whole Church today, not by the contemporary utterances of inspired individuals, but by the teaching and application of the inspired Scriptures he has given us. Some seem to imply or suggest that there may be a leading or guiding of the Spirit that is regardless of the Scriptures. This must be refuted. There is no leading of the Holy Spirit contrary to Scripture. Whenever the Holy Spirit speaks to the Church in the name of the Church's Head, he is always consistent with what he has already revealed.

If we accept the authority of Scripture, we must defer to it, whether it is palatable to human reasoning and contemporary culture or not. We cannot pick and choose what we want to obey, for that is not genuine obedience. The Scriptures must always be allowed to speak the last word on any subject. To discern what that final word is does not release us from the responsibility of understanding the cultural context, and determining the present-day application of commands, instructions and principles directed originally at an immediate situation different from our own.

The Scriptures must have final authority over all personal judgements, even those of the most respected church leaders. The Bereans are commended in the New Testament because they checked out what Paul taught them in order to see that it was in accord with the Scriptures (Acts 17:11). Such an approach is always commendable.

The interpretation of Scripture

To affirm the authority of the Scriptures raises the important matter of their proper interpretation. The Scriptures can be misinterpreted – either deliberately or unconsciously. We may misinterpret them through not understanding them, and particularly through not interpreting them in a way consistent with their context.

Equally perilous is misinterpreting the Scriptures because we read them through the spectacles of our traditions and prejudices. None of us is immune to this peril. We are always in danger of finding in the Scriptures just what we want to find or simply looking for a Scripture to prove our case, rather than allowing the whole teaching of Scripture to mould our thinking and convictions.

To understand and interpret the Scriptures properly we must submit ourselves to their authority and to the Holy Spirit's enlightenment. We must study them carefully using every helpful aid. We must be prepared to discuss issues with those whose understanding is different from our own, and we must honestly listen to what they say with a view to arriving at a right interpretation.

The position at which to aim

The position at which to aim is to accept the final authority of Scripture in all matters of faith and practice (including women's ministry) because no legitimate distinction can be made between God's authority and the authority of his Word.

Where the Scriptures are plain and uncompromising, we must be plain and uncompromising. Where the Scriptures are unclear, we must not be dogmatic. Where Christians come to different conclusions on matters that are uncertain or a matter of genuine Christian debate, we should recognise the right and duty of each believer – or group of believers – to be fully persuaded in their own minds concerning what they should believe and do. We should certainly not allow differences on such secondary issues to divide us or to cause a breakdown in fellowship.

We must discern what are plainly divine *commands* or *imperatives*. We must recognise the difference between biblical *instructions* and *principles*. *Instructions* are to be obeyed and *principles* are to be applied. We must beware of making laws out of our own personal or corporate application of principles.

Many things we all do in our church life appear to bear the character of laws or instructions, but in reality some are simply our application of principles. Think, for instance, of the different ways in which Christians celebrate the Lord's Supper, or the varying procedures in churches for the ordination of ministers. Each Christian group may have rigid rules and regulations; in fact, they are not following New Testament instructions but simply applying principles which allow for great variation in their application. We may fall too easily into the snare of giving to our personal application of principles the authority we should give only to clear instructions of Scripture.

In considering women's ministry, we must be asking first and foremost, 'What is the will of the Head of the Church?' To answer that question we must turn to the Scriptures, submitting ourselves to their authority, being prepared to say 'yes' to whatever they say before we are certain of what they do say on the subject. That is no easy thing to do.

Where clear instructions are given about women's ministry, we must follow them, whether in tune with our age or not. Where principles are laid down, we must endeavour to apply them conscientiously, wherever that may lead us. And since God has always more light to cast upon his Word, change will be necessary in attitudes and actions on the part of us all.

Questions for discussion

1. What gives the Bible its unique authority?

2. What does the Bible's authority mean in practice when we discuss matters which can divide Christians?

3. Can we identify instructions in the Bible which are plainly binding upon all Christians?

4. Can we think of Bible passages which deal with subjects of little contemporary significance, but where principles of permanent validity are established?

Chapter Two

Back to the Beginning – the Book of Genesis

Before trying to suggest ways forward in the debate about women's ministry, we must consider the principal scriptures which are debated, and appreciate why they give rise to so much discussion. We will deal with them in their biblical order so as to make reference back to them easy.

My purpose is to identify the main scriptures, and to establish the things they teach which seem beyond dispute. At the same time I want to draw attention to fundamental questions they present, and identify the principal interpretations and consensus concerning the answers to these questions.

It is not my intention to deal in great detail with the individual scriptures as this has been done almost *ad infinitum*. But consideration of them is fundamental, and the conclusions at which we arrive must determine our views, convictions and actions because of the unique authority the Scriptures have as the Word of God.

Then later I will attempt to put the various conclusions together in a coherent form. At this stage in writing I honestly do not know what those conclusions will be! My determination, as best I am able, is to be freshly open to the Scriptures as we consider them.

The right place to begin

Genesis – the book of beginnings – is the obvious place to start. It describes the creation of man and woman, and God's intentions for their relationship. It then shows how God's good purposes were marred by sin's entry into the world, so that we are now part of a spoiled creation. The unhappy tensions between the sexes stem from our first parents' rebellion against God.

The Book of Genesis is fundamentally important because it is the principal reference point in the New Testament when the relationship of men and women is referred to, by both our Lord Jesus Christ himself and the apostle Paul.

One basic question for which we need an answer is, 'Does the order of God's creation of man and woman have significance?' A further question is, 'Are there essential differences in men and women which from the creation make their natures and gifts different?'

Different but complementary

Man was made in God's image and likeness (1:26) – a spiritual resemblance rather than physical.

24

Man is rational in that he is able to reason (eg 2:19–20), and he is a moral and responsible being. Man's likeness to God was further reflected in the authority given him to rule over the other creatures God had made (1:26).

But in speaking of 'man' we are speaking of male *and* female (1:27), in that male and female *together* were given authority to 'subdue' the earth and to 'rule' all other living creatures (1:28). In creating male and female in his own image, God made humanity bisexual (1:27).

Male and female *together* reflect God's image (1:27) – not simply the male. The first two verses of Genesis 5 confirm this: 'When God created man, he made him in the likeness of God. He created them male and female; at the time they were created, he blessed them and called them "man".' Although Adam bears the name 'man' as the head of the race, it requires both man and woman to express God's image and what it means to be truly human.

God's image is reflected, therefore, in the complementary nature of male and female. God made them different, just as he made male and female different in other species of his creatures. The distinction between men and women is an inbuilt characteristic of humankind as God created it.

We must not pass over the statement that God is said to have 'blessed them' (1:28). We see from 1:22 and 2:3 in the context of creation that for God to bless is for God to define a creature's function and purpose. God blessed man and woman by giving them different but comple-

...unctions. When God declared that all ...had made was very good (1:31), that ...ed the essentially different yet co...ementary features of men's and women's natures.

Whatever conclusions about women's ministry we arrive at, we ought not to base them upon the assumption that men's and women's ministries must be identical. That may be a common attitude of contemporary society, but it is not the Bible's teaching. Men and women are to be plainly acknowledged to be different, and at the same time their individual and separate functions are to be seen as incomplete without those of the other sex. They are certainly not intended to be in opposition to one another or in a position of rivalry. If they are, then we are misunderstanding God's purpose in their creation.

The original harmony of complementarity

The Book of Genesis provides two parallel accounts of creation. The first (1:1–2:3) is a comprehensive description of the whole of creation, with man as its climax. The second focuses upon man's pre-eminence in God's creative purposes (2:4–25). In both accounts the male is mentioned first, and his inherent precedence is implied (1:27; 2:7, 15ff).

Man's defined duty was to work the earth and to take care of it (2:15). He was to develop its potential and protect it from harm and abuse.

At this stage there was no element of difficulty or frustration about his work. Man was to find the enjoyment in his work that God finds in his. One of the first glimpses we are given of Adam's activity is his naming – and thus classifying – all God's living creatures (2:19–20). Besides constituting a highly demanding and scientific task, it implies man's pleasure and delight both in God's work and in his own.

But that actual surveying of God's creation served only to underline that there was no other creature who was an exact complement to man (2:20). Man alone was lonely. Woman was created, therefore, to relieve man's loneliness (2:18). The stress is upon woman being 'a helper suitable' for man (2:18,20). Plainly man was also to be a helper suitable for woman, but the primary emphasis is upon woman's suitability for man.

'A helper suitable for him' is literally 'a help as opposite him' (2:18); that is to say, corresponding to him. She was created to make him complete – once more a stress upon difference but complementarity. The word 'helper' must not be interpreted as implying subordination, as it is also used of God's relationship to man, as in Psalm 33:20: 'We wait in hope for the Lord; he is our help and our shield.'

Woman was created out of man and for that reason she bears God's image as man does (2:21–23). Man was prior to the woman for he was not taken out of her, but she was taken out of him (2:22–23). The way in which woman's creation is described is clearly intended to express woman's dependence upon man, and man's priority or headship in God's ordering of his creation. If Adam's naming of God's creatures in Genesis 2:19–20 was an expression of the headship God gave him over these creatures, then his naming of Eve (2:23) could be an expression likewise of his headship over her, but this is nowhere stated. Name-giving in the Bible does seem to imply some degree of authority of the name-giver over the one named.

Priority, however, is not to be interpreted as meaning superiority. God who created everything is plainly a God of order, and for the well-being of male and female he determined that it should be the male first and the female second. This in no way implies female inferiority. Such a suggestion is never present. In fact one reason for identifying man's priority is to establish his responsibility for caring for the woman and treating her with loving care and respect (cf 1 Pet 3:7).

The man and the woman were in harmony as they appreciated each other and their complementarity. Without the woman the man knew himself to be deficient. Since she had been taken out of him (2:22), he knew himself to be complete only when he was in harmony with her. It was a matter of being in a right relationship with his own flesh. Likewise, without the man the woman was also incomplete: having been taken out of him, she was only complete with him. Together Adam and Eve reflected God's image. Once Eve was taken out of Adam, he no longer perfectly reflected God's image on his own – it was together they reflected his likeness.

Equal but different is the proper conclusion as we survey man and woman as they were first created, with the implicit recognition of man's headship since the woman was created for the man. As together they submitted to God's purpose, they enjoyed harmony.

In the church – as elsewhere – men and women need each other, and God intends them to be complementary in their gifts and personalities. Some gifts and aspects of personality may be the same in the man and in the woman, but not all. They were created to be different. Physical differences between the sexes are matched by differences of gift and personality.

Feminism and the fight for equal rights have tended to obscure the proper and delightful differences there are – and are intended to be – between men and women. Our complementarity as men and women should mean that there is no unhappy rivalry or competition between the sexes. But sadly there is, and that dates back to the fall and the spoiling of the divine image in man and woman.

The sad consequences of the fall

The fall of man (described in Genesis 3) threw a spanner into the works of God's perfect creation. God's image was so spoiled that men and women now need to be renewed in knowledge in the image of their Creator (Col 3:10). Although the primary consequence was man's spoiled relationship with God, the fall also affected every other relationship, and especially the perfect relationship between man and woman.

The woman succumbed first to temptation and disobedience, and she then led her husband into sin (3:6). There was perhaps a certain inevitability about man's succumbing too because of the oneness they possessed. The way in which in Genesis 3:14, 16–17 God addresses first the serpent, then the woman, and finally the man follows the order of events, but because of man's headship, Adam is elsewhere held responsible for the introduction of sin and death to the human race (Rom 5:12).

Their relationship with God was immediately spoiled by their sin: they hid from him (3:8), although such a thought had never before entered their heads. Their relationship with each other lost its naturalness, and unhelpful sexual awareness entered in. The perfect ease they were intended to enjoy was ruined (2:25; cf 3:7). Embarrassment and shame between the sexes appeared, never to disappear. Sadly too the element of blaming others began (3:12).

Genesis 1–3 presents us with basic truths, therefore, which have permanent consequences. Created second, woman sinned first. Intended as a helper for her husband, she instead led him into sin. Genesis 3:6 points out that Adam 'her husband . . . was with her'. Besides being responsible for his own disobedience (Rom 5:12–14), Adam failed to take the lead in doing what was right. The order of events had tragic consequences both for the woman and the man.

Judgement inevitably came upon Adam and Eve (3:16–19). The ideas conveyed by God's judgement upon them are that prior to the fall the woman's principal task was child-bearing (and by implication the care of the family) and man's was work (and by implication providing for the family). These characteristic tasks were not altered by the fall but sadly marred.

Woman's child-bearing had an element of increased pain added to it (3:16). At this stage Adam is said to have named his wife Eve (ie living) 'because she would become the mother of all the living' (3:20). In place of an understanding and intelligent submission to her husband, the wife's submission tends to be characterised either by the desire to reverse roles or by a sometimes unjust subjection. If the word 'desire' in Genesis 3:16 is translated in the same way as in Genesis 4:7, the implication is that the woman has the same desire for her husband that sin had for Cain – a desire to master and control him. The man's task is to see that this does not happen.

This interpretation may not be very palatable today but it has a ring of truth about it. Instead of headship being a matter of love and submission (as God originally intended), it is now a matter of struggle and conflict. If this interpretation of 'desire' is correct, then women's desire to reverse divinely established

31

roles and to master men is a direct consequence of the fall – and one to be resisted. In place of the mutual help which God purposed, there is an element of hostility.

As a result of the fall man rules over woman in a way that was not true beforehand (3:16). By taking the initiative in eating of the tree of the knowledge of good and evil, the woman in effect assumed the leadership role, contrary to God's will and with disastrous results. As a consequence, the man now is to be clearly in the position of leadership. While not defined, woman's relationship to man has an element of bondage added to it as a result of the fall (3:16). Unfortunately, the fall means that man in his sinfulness often wrongly interprets headship as domination.

It would seem that all the time their relationship to God was right, there was no need for any emphasis upon the principles of male rule and female submission. They rejoiced in loving and serving one another, and found satisfaction in each other's different gifts and natures. When sin entered in, however, so did the need to articulate and teach the principles of rule and submission. And that situation remains.

Although new birth, and the new creation of which it is part, introduces wonderful changes, they do not mean that we lose our sinful natures. The principles of rule and submission continue until our final redemption, when there will be neither male nor female as we now know them (Mt 22:30).

Man's pre-eminent task of work (3:17–19), as

the breadwinner, has elements of pain, drudgery and futility about it as a consequence of the fall. Work had been planned for him previously (2:15), but now painful labour characterises it.

The conclusion seems inescapable that there is profound significance in the order of creation for determining the proper relationship between the sexes. Man has priority, not in the sense that he is superior to the woman, but because God has ordained man to be the leader and the provider. Men and women are not to view themselves as rivals but as complementary – as needing one another for completeness. This is true not only in marriage, but in all other aspects of their relationships. The gifts and personalities of men and women match and complement each other.

In our modern society we have chosen to put aside these broad principles, and sometimes to ignore or reverse them altogether. From simple observation it is questionable if this has been the progress that has been sometimes claimed. From the viewpoint of the Scriptures, to ignore these principles is simply to perpetuate men's and women's rebellion against their Creator's plan and to forfeit the blessing he intends them to know through mutual dependence and natural complementarity.

Questions for discussion

1. Does the order of God's creation of men and women matter?

2. Are there essential differences in men and women which from the creation make their natures and gifts different? If so, name some of them.

3. Do we sense any feeling of unhelpful rivalry between the sexes within the church? If so, is it because some have the conviction that male and female functions should be the same?

4. Are there illustrations we can give to demonstrate that priority does not automatically mean superiority?

Chapter Three

Paul's Vital Contribution

Most discussions about women's ministry in the church centre on the apostle Paul's instructions, and especially on what he says about public teaching and the exercise of authority. We cannot arrive at proper conclusions about women's ministry, therefore, and decisions as to necessary change in the church, without understanding what he teaches.

Some have suggested that Paul was prejudiced against women, and have even described him as a woman-hater. This is to malign Paul. As we read his letters we see how quick he is to draw attention to his female fellow-workers, and he warmly commends them. Outstanding was Phoebe, who had been 'a great help to many people', including Paul himself (Rom 16:1–2). The word translated 'help' is the word 'servant' or 'deacon' as used elsewhere in the New Testament (eg, Phil 1:1). Women like Euodia and Syntyche are described as having contended at his side in the cause of the gospel (Phil 4:2–3). Women figure prominently in the list of his colleagues in Romans 16:3–23.

Much has been made of Paul being simply a man of his day in what he says about women's place in the church. The suggestion is that he was biased on account of the culture and customs of the society of which he was part.

It would be foolish to deny that Paul was a man of his times, just as we too are influenced by our own contemporary society. But alongside this we must place the fundamental truth that Paul was a specially chosen apostle of Jesus Christ. As such he was inspired by the Spirit of Christ as he taught the churches and as he wrote the letters we now find in the New Testament. He was pleased when people checked out what he said by the Scriptures that they already possessed (Acts 17:11; 1 Cor 4:6), but he was in no doubt about his apostolic authority.

Whenever we proclaim the gospel of Christ, we invariably, although perhaps sometimes unconsciously, lean heavily upon Paul's exposition of it in the New Testament, and rightly so. There is no logical reason why we should accept the authority of what he says about the gospel, and then ignore what he says about church practice.

Paul 'wrote . . . with the wisdom that God gave him' (2 Pet 3:15). That is not to say that all he wrote is crystal clear on every subject, and the Scriptures themselves recognise this, for as Peter says, 'His letters contain some things that are hard to understand' (2 Pet 3:16).

It has also been suggested that what Paul said – although inspired and written with apostolic authority – was relevant only to his immediate situation. This suggestion may be accepted as valid on those few occasions where Paul indicates that such may have been the case, as in 1 Corinthians 7:25ff and 40. However, where no such qualification is made, we must accept what he says about other issues – including women's ministry in the church – as carrying the same authority as what he says about the gospel itself.

The key passages in the present debate – in the order in which they appear in the New Testament – are 1 Corinthians 11:2–16, 1 Corinthians 14:33–38 and 1 Timothy 2:11–15. Galatians 3:26–29 must also be considered as it is sometimes quoted in the contemporary discussion of women's ministry, together with 1 Timothy 3:11 with its possible reference to deaconesses.

My intention is not to attempt an exhaustive exposition of these passages since numerous attempts have been made to do this. It is plain that precise interpretation at some points where views vary is not possible because we are not in a position to compare scripture with scripture. My purpose is to indicate their context, and to pinpoint the key questions the passages raise and to endeavour to answer them.

Acceptable behaviour in church services (1 Cor 11:2–16)

²I praise you for remembering me in everything and for holding to the teachings, just as I passed them on to you.
³Now I want you to realise that the head of every man is Christ, and the head of the woman

is man, and the head of Christ is God. [4]Every man who prays or prophesies with his head covered dishonours his head. [5]And every woman who prays or prophesies with her head uncovered dishonours her head – it is just as though her head were shaved. [6]If a woman does not cover her head, she should have her hair cut off; and if it is a disgrace for a woman to have her hair cut or shaved off, she should cover her head. [7]A man ought not to cover his head, since he is the image and glory of God; but the woman is the glory of man. [8]For the man did not come from the woman, but woman from man; [9]neither was man created for woman, but woman for man. [10]For this reason, and because of the angels, the woman ought to have a sign of authority on her head.

[11]In the Lord, however, woman is not independent of man, nor is man independent of woman. [12]For as woman came from man, so also man is born of woman. But everything comes from God. [13]Judge for yourselves: Is it proper for a woman to pray to God with her head uncovered? [14]Does not the very nature of things teach you that if a man has long hair, it is a disgrace to him, [15]but that if a woman has long hair, it is her glory? For long hair is given to her as a covering. [16]If anyone wants to be contentious about this, we have no other practice – nor do the churches of God.

The wider context of this passage provides an important key to the right approach to the whole subject of women's ministry.

Paul has been discussing a believer's freedom. Some at Corinth had obviously been quoting and acting upon a saying common among Christians, 'Everything is permissible.' Sadly, however, they did so in a way that was liable to bring Christian conduct into disrepute. Paul counters this false emphasis by saying, ' "Everything is permissible" – but not everything is beneficial. "Everything is permissible" – but not everything is constructive' (1 Cor 10:23).

His pastoral concern was that the Corinthians' behaviour should honour God by not causing anyone to stumble, 'whether Jews, Greeks or the church of God' (1 Cor 10:32).

Having said this, he moves on to deal with acceptable behaviour in church services. The implication is that by stressing the rightful principle of Christian freedom here as in every other sphere, they had gone to extremes and were behaving in a manner which could cause both Christians and non-Christians to be upset and offended.

The issue which gave rise at this point to the teaching about the relationship of men and women is head-covering in corporate worship – a subject which seems remote from us.

The alternative text of verses 4–7 – given at the bottom of the page in the New International Version – suggests that the issue is a matter of hair-styles rather than of head-covering, such as a veil in the first century or a hat at the present time. While some would argue for this alternative, what we know of first-century culture makes a reference to a veil or head-covering much more appropriate.

It would appear that head-covering had not been a subject upon which Paul had cause to say much, if anything at all, while he was in Corinth because he commends the Corinthians for remembering him in everything and for holding to the teachings, just as he passed them on to them (v 2). It seems to have become a difficulty after he had left them, and news of the problem had reached him.

Some women at Corinth took part in public worship by praying and prophesying (v 5). This is to be censured in 14:34–35, but Paul wisely deals with only one subject at a time, and we likewise shall consider this later. What had disturbed some was that they took part without having their heads covered. We may make a reasonable guess as to the reason.

The first converts in Corinth were undoubtedly Jews and God-fearers (Gentiles who had accepted the Jewish faith) – see Acts 18:4–8. Such automatically carried over their synagogue customs into Christian worship. But then the church had also welcomed into its fellowship many Gentiles who had no Jewish background. It was probably some of these Gentile women Christians who worshipped without a head-covering.

On being challenged about it, they may reasonably have asked, 'Why should we cover our heads? Is there anything in the Scriptures about it? What did our Lord Jesus say? What did Paul teach?' Such questions may have drawn a blank, and they may have concluded that it was simply a Jewish custom with no relevance to Christians. They may have felt this all the more strongly since Paul clearly did not teach that men should continue the

Jewish practice of having their heads covered.

The New International Version appropriately entitles this section of the letter 'Propriety in Worship'. When we observe a propriety we recognise that there is a way of doing things which is acceptable to others, and which we ought not to ignore unless there is good reason for doing so. If this passage is to be considered in the light of 1 Corinthians 10:31f – as I think it is – then Jews and Greeks, as well as the Church of God generally, considered it appropriate for women to have their heads covered.

The covering of the head in the first century – or the wearing of a veil – was vastly different from wearing a hat today. Corinth was notorious for loose living and immorality. One of the marks of a prostitute in Corinth was an uncovered head, although Paul does not give that as the reason for what he says. When a woman covered her head in the Orient she was given respect and shown courtesy. Christian women in Corinth who ignored the propriety of a head-covering probably gave a false impression concerning the nature of their Christian freedom, and may well have been a stumbling block to others.

Furthermore, in first-century Corinth a woman's covering of her head was a symbol of her recognition of the authority of the man (v 10), and in particular her husband. It is not such in the late twentieth century in the West. Our responsibility, therefore, is to discern the principle behind the instruction about head-coverings. The application of the principle – it would seem to me, therefore – is that a wife should consult her husband's preference, and that an unmarried woman should do what is accepted practice in that part of God's family with which she is identified.

In secondary matters like this, we are to behave according to the proper conventions of our day, aiming to give no unnecessary offence to anyone, and so live to God's glory (1 Cor 10:31–32).

Our interest in this whole passage is that Paul reinforces what he says by speaking clearly about God's intentions for the relationship of the two sexes, and in doing so he goes back to Genesis 1–3, the place where we ourselves have begun.

Paul indicates in a rather gentle fashion that in what he is about to say he is sure that he is following the example of Christ (11:1). We ought not to miss the significance of this. If we follow Paul's instruction, therefore, we will find ourselves safely following Christ.

Paul lifts the whole subject onto the highest level by beginning with Christ himself (v 3). Our first reaction to what he writes about him may be one of surprise because plainly our Lord Jesus Christ is equal with the Father, being of one essence with him and the Holy Spirit. But Paul has in view our Lord's becoming subject to the Father in our human flesh in order to be our Mediator. He draws attention to the subjection of Jesus Christ to the Father because he wants to affirm and illustrate the nature of the woman's subjection to the man. 'Now I want you to realise,' he says, 'that the head of every man is Christ, and the head of the woman is man, and the head of Christ is God' (v 3).

God is a God of order – a truth we may observe both in God's activity in creation and in his plan of salvation. Since he is a God of order, there is a proper order in human relationships, and an appropriate way of doing things.

God's order in creating man first was not an accident but God's deliberate purpose. It is God's will, therefore, that the woman should acknowledge God's purpose and recognise man's proper headship. She is to be subject to the man as he is to be subject to Christ. Whatever our culture, and whatever the contemporary trends may be, this purpose of God must be recognised and applied. The order is not the consequence of the fall but of creation. Rule and submission were there from creation. The fall meant that they were resented and needed to be spelled out.

But subordination is not to be interpreted as meaning inferiority. To emphasise this Paul underlines Christ's subordination to the Father – 'the head of Christ is God' (v 3). As we have said, God is not Christ's Head in regard to his divine nature, but in regard to his office and work as Mediator. Man is the head of the woman, not because their essential natures are different, but because God has set the man over the woman in the functions he is to fulfil – for her benefit as much as his own.

Some argue that the word 'head' is interpreted

simply as implying source or origin – an interpretation which is quite legitimate in terms of classical Greek's use of the word. But it is hard to imagine Paul writing of God being the 'origin' of Christ. Post-Septuagint usage seems clearly to imply the element of authority to which submission is necessary.

Admittedly in everyday speech subjection tends to be equated with inferiority, but that is not the case here. The Son is equal with the Father, although subject to him. Men and women are equal in the sight of God, although the woman is to be subordinate to the man. The Son submits himself gladly to the Father. Likewise, when man behaves properly, he submits himself gladly to Christ, and woman similarly to man. The Son's equality with the Father does not mean that they fulfil identical functions. Similarly, the equality of men and women does not mean that they carry out the same functions. Although Christ's headship expresses the truth of his authority over the Church, it is important to remember that his headship is at the same time exemplary, protective and practical (Eph 5:22–33).

Paul confirms what he says in verse 3 by further references in verses 7, 8, 11–12 to God's intentions. Man 'is the image and glory of God; but the woman is the glory of man' (v 7). The man is to behave always in the light of his relationship to God, and the woman is to behave always in the light of her creation to be man's partner. 'Man did not come from woman, but woman from man; neither was man created for woman, but woman for man' (vv 8–9). They are intended, therefore, to be partners, not rivals. Their proper partnership depends upon the recognition of the order God intends in their relationship.

Contemporary thought suggests that men and women can in many ways live without one another, and that equality means that conventions and proprieties about relationships between the sexes may be abandoned. Sometimes the suggestion is made – either in what is said or more pointedly in how Christians behave – that conversion and being united to Christ mean that these distinctions between the sexes may cease, and should, in effect, be nullified. (We shall look at this more closely when we consider Galatians 3:26–29.)

Such views are refuted by Paul in verses 11–12. Our being 'in the Lord' does not alter the original order that God established for his creation, and thus for male-female relationships. In fact, being 'in the Lord' should mean that we better fulfil his original purposes in these relationships since they were 'very good' from the outset (Gen 1:31). Reconciled to God, with the mind of Christ increasingly in us, the effort to dominate and exploit – one of the sad legacies of the fall – will be restrained and corrected.

Man's dependence upon woman is as great as her dependence upon him for 'as woman came from man, so also man is born of woman' (v 12). God has made this true so that men and women in marriage, in human society and in the Church, should properly complement one another.

The right order of things is not in conflict with equality and mutual dependence. We are to accept this principle of subordination in the whole of life, including church services. We might also add that these harmonious attitudes should be displayed especially in and by the Church. The members of the body of Christ – those who are 'in the Lord' (v 11) and thus in a right relationship with him – should be showing to the world what the proper relationship between the sexes ought to be. Paul concludes by stressing that 'everything comes from God' (v 12) – that is to say, he is the One who has ordered the way thngs are and he is the One we should obey.

Paul recognised that some might want to argue over this whole matter, and that in itself is not insignificant in view of today's debate. His answer is that the principles he has outlined are those that guide his own and others' practice, in all the churches (v 16).

It is interesting that Paul mentions the 'practice' (v 16) of the churches. Over the course of nearly two thousand years, Christians have arrived at clear decisions about the application of biblical and spiritual principles regarding the respective ministries of men and women. These decisions, while not by any means infallible, are not to be despised. They are to be tested by Scripture – not by contemporary fashions. Where they prove to be a genuine application of biblical principles they are to be followed; where they are not, they are to be discarded.

Those who choose to discard long-standing

practices which are true to Scripture soon lose their way and become subject to constant winds of change. As Dean Inge expressed it, 'He who marries the spirit of the age will soon find himself a widower.'

Early church practice (1 Cor 14:33b–38)

33b As in all the congregations of the saints, 34 women should remain silent in the churches. They are not allowed to speak, but must be in submission, as the Law says. 35 If they want to enquire about something, they should ask their own husbands at home; for it is disgraceful for a woman to speak in the church.

These verses are part of a passage appropriately entitled in the New International Version 'Orderly Worship'. An element of disorder had entered the life of the Corinthian church through too many people wanting to exercise spoken ministry at one and the same time, whether by the choice of a hymn, the giving of a word of instruction or of revelation (presumably by prophecy) or an interpretation. Because 'God is not a God of disorder but of peace' (v 33), Paul argues for order and discipline when God's people come together for worship and instruction. 'Everything should be done in a fitting and orderly way' (v 40).

It is in this context that Paul immediately underlines the general practice of all the early congregations that women should remain silent in the churches (33–34), when the whole church comes together for worship and instruction. The implication is that this applies to the contribution of 'a hymn, or a word of instruction, a revelation, a tongue or an interpretation' (v 26). The asking of questions about what has been taught or prophesied is also included (v 35).

We are bound to ask, 'Is Paul expressing a purely personal conviction? Is this just first-century culture that he is reflecting?' On consideration of the passage, the answer has to be 'no'. First, he refers specifically to the practice of 'all the congregations of the saints' (v 33). Other apostles had been involved in the establishment of such churches, besides the apostle Paul, and the practice with regard to women's ministry was identical in those churches too.

Secondly, he goes back to Scripture – to the Law (v 34). He probably refers primarily to God's words to the woman, following the fall, in Genesis 3:16b: 'Your desire will be for your husband, and he will rule over you.' Woman's proper place, as with the man's, is to be determined by Scripture, not by culture. Women are not to speak in public worship services as an expression of their submission both to God and to man – to God because it is his instruction to them, and to man because it is God's will.

We are left, however, with the question of what Paul had in mind in 1 Corinthians 11:5 where he mentions women who prophesied, as indeed we know Philip's daughters did (Acts 21:9). Did he consider that there were exceptional occasions when women might prophesy in the context of a meeting of the church? The answer is that we do not know. What we may say is that when we lay down principles – as Paul does – we do not lay down hard and fast rules to which there are no exceptions. Sometimes, for example, principles may conflict, in which case the higher must prevail. Both are good, but when both cannot be achieved at the same time, the higher must take priority over the principle of lesser importance.

There may be circumstances – as sometimes in missionary work today – where women are placed in situations where men ought to be, and where the ideal cannot be practised, although it can and should be aimed at.

The gift of prophecy clearly did not have to be exercised only in the context of church services. It could be exercised, for example, in the home and in the spontaneous coming together of Christians within a home. We are not told, for instance, that Philip's daughters (Acts 21:8–9) exercised their ministry in public worship. It could also be exercised by women when they came together among themselves for mutual encouragement and fellowship.

Since Paul points out that 'the spirits of prophets are subject to the control of prophets' (v 32), he may have envisaged a woman having the gift of prophecy, and her exercising it in public, when both men and women were present, if asked by those whose reponsibility it was to direct the corporate worship of God's people. She would then be exercising it in the context of submission.

There is also the possibility that prophecy was regarded as intrinsically different from teaching, and that for a woman to exercise that gift was not seen to be in conflict with the principle that the preaching and teaching function should be with men. These all seem possible explanations.

But however we interpret the uncertainties of 1 Corinthians 11:5, we must interpret it by the plain statements Paul makes elsewhere. With the renewed mention of 'submission' (v 34), we must remind ourselves that submission is not inferiority, since, as we have seen, our Lord Jesus Christ submits himself to the Father, and his submission is the model for ours.

Not all at Corinth, however, accepted these principles, and it was for this reason Paul asked, 'Did the word of God originate with you? Or are you the only people it has reached?' (v 36). Some of the Corinthians acted in these matters as if they could behave independently of the rest of the church and also of apostolic guidance. Paul did not often resort to spelling out his apostolic authority, but he does so on this occasion (vv 37–38). It must be highly significant and relevant to our present discussion of women's ministry that he actually says that what he writes is 'the Lord's command' (v 37), and that those possessing spiritual discernment would recognise this to be the case.

While Paul does not say as much about women's ministry as perhaps we would wish, and there are some questions we cannot answer, the plain implication of this passage, as with the previous one, is that in services of worship and instruction, where both sexes are present, women should not participate publicly in the teaching ministry. Behind this instruction is the order God has laid down, both in creation itself and then after the fall.

As I hinted earlier, this principle regarding the public ministry of women to both sexes has often had to be put aside in missionary situations because of a lack of men. I find no problem with this, because God does not limit his blessing to ideal situations. If he did, then we might not know any blessing at all in our churches! Furthermore, as previously suggested, when two principles conflict, the higher must prevail. The principle that a man should engage in the public teaching of the gospel is still a principle, even if it has to be subordinated in a particular situation to the higher principle that the gospel must be taken to every nation. This is relevant to many aspects of missionary work throughout the world.

Women who find themselves in such positions usually exercise their ministry because they have been asked to do so by those who have leadership over them. Hopefully such women's desire is to see a national leadership raised up which conforms better to the biblical ideal, thus enabling them to do other equally necessary tasks more consistent with the biblical pattern.

Where we can apply the principles we know to be right, we are to do so. Where we cannot, then we must work towards those situations in which we can, remembering that we are talking about principles rather than rules.

Our aim and purpose is not to do simply what is *permissible*, but to aim at what is *beneficial* and *constructive*, seeking not what we want, but what is best for all and above all pleasing to God (1 Cor 10:23–24).

Instruction concerning public teaching (1 Tim 2:11–15)

[11]A woman should learn in quietness and full submission. [12]I do not permit a woman to teach or to have authority over a man; she must be silent. [13]For Adam was formed first, then Eve. [14]And Adam was not the one deceived; it was the woman who was deceived and became a sinner. [15]But women will be saved through childbirth, if they continue in faith, love and holiness with propriety.

1 Timothy 2:11–15 is probably the clearest of the three principal passages we are considering in the directions that it gives, although it too raises questions we cannot answer with certainty.

Paul's purpose in writing to Timothy was that he should know 'how people ought to conduct themselves in God's household' (1 Tim 3:15). This helps us to answer the question as to how normative Paul's instructions here are intended to be. The verb he uses, translated 'ought', indicates a strong degree of necessity. The instructions have relevance beyond Timothy's immediate situation.

He begins with a clear and unequivocal instruction that women 'should learn in quietness and full submission' (v 11). The mention of learning in quietness ties in with the instruction of 1 Corinthians 14:35 that 'if they want to enquire about something, they should ask their own husbands at home'. Submission is likewise found in 1 Corinthians 14:34 where Paul establishes it to be mandatory on account of God's Law.

What is new in this passage is the direct instruction that in the church a woman should neither teach nor have authority over a man (v 12). These two directives have been implied in the previous passages, but here they are plainly stated. Teaching in church services of both sexes together is a male function, and so too is the exercise of spiritual authority.

Paul immediately goes on to relate these directives to Genesis 1–3, as he did by implication in 1 Corinthians 14:34 also.

It has been perhaps natural for the suggestion to be made that the instructions of verses 11–12 arose out of the cultural background of Paul's day or some particular circumstance of the time. But Paul carefully lifts the subject above such an interpretation by his reference to God's creative purpose (v 13) and the consequences of sin's entry into the world (v 14). Had Paul not written like this, we might well have inferred that local or temporary circumstances dictated his directives. But such seems to be ruled out by his renewed reference to Genesis 1–3. He argues not from culture, but from Scripture.

The manner in which Paul expresses the grounds for his directives in verses 11–12 bears the echoes of Genesis 3: sin entered the world when woman broke out of the pattern God had established by leading rather than following the man. This in no way absolved the man from his responsibility for his sin, but sin did enter the world through an improper reversal of God-given roles. The right order of things is to be followed by Christians, and one of the principal spheres of that recognition of God's order is in public worship and instruction. Here the general principle is that the man is to lead, and the woman is to follow.

Reference must be made to verse 15 because it is a problem verse on account of there being no parallel or similar statements by which we may interpret it. The interpretation that seems to make best sense, and to fit the context, links it with the preceding verse. The word 'women' is in fact – as a marginal reference will probably make plain – the word 'she', which in terms of verse 14 makes the reference to be to Eve first and then to all women (note the 'they' of the verb 'continue'). The promise that the seed of the woman would ultimately bruise the head of the serpent was given particularly to Eve in God's statement to the serpent in Genesis 3:15.

This became the great Old Testament hope. At God's chosen time a woman – a virgin – gave birth to a son, the Saviour of the world. The woman – as well as the man – is saved by this unique child-bearing, for the Saviour was born through her. The woman's role in God's plan of salvation, therefore, has been vital. Her submissive role in relation to the man, therefore, is not to be interpreted to mean that she is in any way a kind of 'second-class citizen'. But this salvation is the experience only of those who trust in Christ, and who hold fast to that faith with love and holiness – and, significantly, in the context of women's ministry – a holiness that does not despise propriety.

It has been suggested that Paul does not have in mind women being saved either from judgement or from death in childbirth, but rather their being kept safe from wrongly seizing men's roles by embracing a woman's role – symbolised here by childbirth – accompanied by other evidences of Christian character like 'faith, love and holiness' (v 15). This interpretation has in its favour its unity with the context in that it fits well into what Paul is saying in the previous verses. Significantly, the NIV margin note is that 'saved' could be translated 'restored', a word consistent with this interpretation. As redeemed women major on fulfilling their feminine roles, so what was lost at the fall is recovered.

The difficulties we may have in understanding this verse, however, have no particular bearing upon the interpretation of the previous verses in the directives they give about the principles relating to teaching and to rule.

WOMEN IN THE CHURCH

God's equal welcome to men and women (Gal 3:28)

> There is neither Jew nor Greek, slave nor free, male nor female, for you are all one in Christ Jesus.

While Paul's statement here does not strictly deal with women's ministry, and does not occur in a passage relating to the subject, it is often quoted when women's ministry is under discussion, and so must be considered.

The words 'There is neither Jew nor Greek, slave nor free, male nor female, for you are all one in Christ Jesus' occur in a passage in which Paul discusses the means by which God justifies us, establishing that it is through faith in our Lord Jesus Christ alone, and not by works of the law. Furthermore, God deals with all men and women on the same basis, so that in Christ 'there is neither Jew nor Greek, slave nor free, male nor female'. Dealt with in the same way by God, we are one in Christ.

The question must be asked: 'Is Paul by this statement setting aside all distinctions between the sexes in the fellowship of God's people?' The answer must be plainly 'no' since Paul, who is obviously the best interpreter of his own words, recognises the distinction elsewhere in what he writes about the relationship between the sexes, and their function in the church. A basic principle of biblical interpretation is the understanding of one part of Scripture by another, and not least when the writer is the same.

Some suggest that this scripture means that because Christians are rescued from sin and the consequences of the fall, Christian women are rescued from subordination and restored to an equality God originally intended for them. But this is not a justified interpretation.

In terms of access to God, and appropriation of all the benefits of salvation, men and women are absolutely equal in God's sight – and equally welcomed as his spiritual children as they believe on his Son. But just as – to quote this same passage – a slave did not cease to be a slave, or a Jew or Greek cease to be a Jew or Greek when converted, so men and women do not cease to exercise their different yet complementary functions because of their new relationship to God and to one another through Christ. In fact, in the church, we should see men and women living together in harmony as they fulfil and practise their different functions and gifts.

Wives or women deacons? (1 Tim 3:11)

In the same way, their wives are to be women worthy of respect, not malicious talkers but temperate and trustworthy in everything.

There is no discussion in the present debate so far as I know about the first seven verses of this chapter regarding elders in that the requirements clearly relate only to men. But this is obviously not the case in verse 11.

Considerable – and unresolved – debate surrounds the identity of the women referred to in this verse in that the word translated 'wives' can mean women or wives.

Most versions suggest that it is the wives of deacons who are in view, but at the same time give the footnote 'deaconesses'. Whether deacons' wives or not, they may well have been assistants to the deacons when women's needs required looking after. It is possible that Phoebe, whose ministry is described in Romans 16:1, fell into this category, although the word translated there as 'a servant' or 'deaconess' does not necessarily indicate that she held a defined office. It could simply mean that she was conspicuous for her unstinting service. Extra-biblical material suggests that she was prominent – 'known not only to the Greeks and Romans but also to the Barbarians' (Theodoret).

If the reference is to deacons' wives, it is strange that Paul did not give similar instruction concerning elders' wives prior to writing about deacons. It could be argued, however, that Paul refers to the wives of both elders and deacons at this point.

If – as seems to have been the case – responsibilities for teaching and rule were seen as belonging to the men who were called to be elders, and administration and practical caring ministries were the delegated functions of the deacons, there may well have been both men and women who 'served' in these practical ways, and were deacons or deaconesses.

If there is a place for women deacons or deaconesses in accordance with the manner in which this verse is interpreted, it is plain that Paul did not anticipate women as elders. If there are ministries for which men are particularly suited, so too there are ministries for which women are much better suited than men. But the debate about this verse will doubtless go on, and continue to be unresolved.

I freely admit that because of our backgrounds none of us can come to any of these passages with complete objectivity. I am aware too that there are many technical and ingenious interpretations given to some of these passages which result in meanings completely opposite sometimes to the apparent plain meaning of the Scriptures as they stand. Although I accept that some may be helpful insights, when it turns out that every straightforward statement of Scripture is challenged in this way, I am suspicious. God has not put the understanding of his truth only into the hands of those who understand the technicalities of Hebrew and Greek. The 'expert' may say, for example, that 'head' does not mean 'head' as we are in the habit of using the word. But, in fact, the experts themselves differ on this, as they do in other matters. God has not left essential truth in jeopardy of differing linguistic interpretations.

Questions for discussion

1. How common is it for Christians to argue for what is beneficial or constructive rather than for what is merely permissible? Can we give practical illustrations of the application of this principle?

2. How would we illustrate male and female complementarity?

3. In what ways can it be demonstrated that submission or subordination are not to be automatically interpreted as inferiority?

4. What do Romans 16 and Philippians 4:2–3 say and imply about Paul's appreciation of women's partnership in the work of the gospel?

5. How can the Church uniquely demonstrate what the proper relationship between the sexes should be?

★ ★ ★ ★

HOTEL BAHIA

Avenida Alfonso XIII, 6
Teléfs. 221700 - 221750 (10 lineas)
Telex 35859
S A N T A N D E R

<u>N O T A S</u>

Chapter Four

Putting the Jigsaw Together Without All the Pieces

This chapter's title expresses both the situation as I see it, and the task in which we must now engage. We do not have a complete picture of women's ministry in the church during the New Testament period. Nevertheless, having in mind the picture of a jigsaw, we possess the majority of the pieces, and have sufficient to make sense of it, and probably enough to fill in fairly accurately the pieces that are missing.

In the previous two chapters we concentrated upon clear statements of Scripture rather than observations upon biblical narrative. A general principle of biblical interpretation – and obviously a wise one as we ponder it – is that we are to be guided by biblical instructions rather than by any assumptions we may make on the basis of our personal observations about what we feel narrative parts of the Scriptures may teach.

In other words, our understanding of women's ministry is to be moulded by what the Scriptures plainly declare rather than what we might choose to conclude about women's ministry from, say – to take an extreme example – the woman of Samaria's activity in telling the people of the town about the One in whom they might find salvation (Jn 4:29).

The first chapters of Genesis are crucial, not only because they describe God's original and continuing purpose for male-female relationships, but because they are referred to by the apostle Paul – either directly or indirectly – each time he deals with the subject of women in the church (1 Cor 11:2–16; 14:33b–38; 1 Tim 2:11–15).

What picture then does the incomplete jigsaw present? From the beginning it is clear that God is the God of order – everything in the natural world points to that. There is a divinely intended order in the creation of male and then female. This sequence was not a mistake; and it was not something to which God gave significance as an after-thought. Men and women are equal in value and as persons, but different and distinct in the roles they are to play.

The leadership role in general is with the male rather than the female. Sadly, the fall itself took place when Eve chose to reverse this divinely established principle – a principle established by God for the good of humankind.

The leadership role rests with the male because of the essential differences in men and women's natures; differences which God purposefully created. It was essential to God's blessing of male and female that he gave them different but complementary functions.

The male's primary function is to work – to be the provider. The female's primary function is to care for the family. This statement of priority functions does not exclude other functions by either, but it is important to hold on to what is primary because we have often lost sight of this in contemporary society. I recognise that this is not going to be a popular statement. Our present lifestyle, influenced as it is by factors such as high mortgages and house prices, means that both partners in a marriage often go out to work.

Some even reject marriage because they are content to live as husband and wife without the formal contract of marriage. Women in such relationships will understandably be reluctant to give up their employment and careers since they lack – probably unconsciously – the security and stability God intends they should have in a settled marriage relationship.

The leadership/headship role of the male is not meant to imply the inferiority of the female – in fact, far from it. Paul lifts the relationship of male and female to its highest level by reminding us of the divine relationships within the Trinity. The precedence of the Father in the order of the Trinity in no way implies or infers the inferiority of the Son or the Holy Spirit.

Men and women are different, and are divinely intended to be different. Because the whole issue of equality between the sexes is under such continual debate, and because through human perversity male dominance has been taken to extremes, the tendency has been to stress that male and female are completely identical, simply to reinforce the arguments for equal treatment.

Men and women are equal – equal in their standing before God as human beings, and equal as the objects of God's concern and love. Nevertheless, they are different. In fact, their difference is part of the delightful chemistry of human relationships which adds colour and pleasure to life.

Even as male and female are the same yet different physically, biologically and temperamentally, so too they are the same yet different in their functions in society, the family and the body of Christ. Some things they may both do, and other things one may do better than the other. In yet other spheres one may be plainly cut out to be and do something which is virtually impossible to the other. Partnership does not mean fulfilling the same roles.

No sense of unhelpful rivalry, therefore, should exist between the sexes. Equal but complementary is the best summary of God's intention. This purpose of God preceded Adam and Eve's rebellion against him. The fall, which tragically spoiled God's perfect creation to the detriment of every part, had harmful effects on male-female harmony.

The fact that the woman sinned first seems to have some bearing on woman's present subordinate function. Her subordination – present before the fall – was increased following her disobedience to God, although not in any way diminishing her equality or complementarity to man. Man's responsibility to be the basic provider or breadwinner was also adversely affected by the fall, and the element of sweat and toil entered into his work.

Man's duty is to 'rule' or 'lead' and woman's duty is to follow – not in a servile manner, but in recognition of necessary order and complementary responsibilities. The danger is that this differentiation can become an excuse for male domination. But the emphasis in Genesis 2 is upon the need which male and female have of each other. As the woman was taken out of the man and belongs to him, so the man is incomplete without the woman. Together they reflect God's image – not man on his own, or the woman on her own, but together.

Throughout the Old Testament God's people recognised male responsibility to lead, whether in God's establishment of the priesthood or in the appointment of kings (eg, Saul and David), or in the raising up of prophets. The exception of someone like Deborah is helpful because it reminds us that principles are not applied in Scripture with the rigidity of rules or laws.

Linked with 'ruling' and 'leading' is teaching. Those who teach do in a sense rule because they uniquely influence lives and behaviour. In the Old Testament the teaching function belonged primarily to the priests and the prophets. The primary influence of women over children in the most important sphere of the home was recognised and honoured.

In the New Testament we see the basic principles of the Old Testament continued. Our Lord Jesus Christ was the most radical teacher ever, and he brought about a revolution in the treatment of women. He not only had time for them and taught them – something totally untypical and unusual about teachers in first-century Judaism – but he involved them in his ministry.

But he did not call any women to be apostles. It might be argued that he was simply following the culture of his day. But the Lord Jesus Christ never followed the culture of his day where it conflicted with truth.

The New Testament spells out two functions as the distinctive responsibility of the male: rule (ie leadership) and teaching. Issues like this are normally dealt with in the New Testament because the matters under discussion were debated, or because established principles were under threat. This may well be the reason for their mention in the New Testament where reference to them is found.

The teaching function is to be exercised by gifted men in the church when both men and women are together. In practice this means, therefore, that eldership (spiritual rule) should be male and that those who teach and preach for the benefit of the whole fellowship of God's people should be male also. This does not exclude exceptional circumstances when a woman may be asked by the eldership to address a congregation, or where a lack of men may mean that women have to step in to fulfil functions temporarily for the benefit of the body, which men usually fulfil.

Sadly, we have got ourselves into an either/or situation. Because women are not meant to rule or teach men, women may then fail to fulfil

these functions at all, especially to those of their
own sex. This is plainly wrong.

We need to remind ourselves that the
establishing of principles is not the same as the
laying down of rules. Principles must not be
interpreted with the legalism associated with
laws.

Women may teach women, and, sadly and
tragically, the gifts of those who possess this
ability have been generally neglected in the
Church. This should be put right, and we must
explore this area of deficiency diligently in order
to do so. Women should be involved in, if not
responsible for, the pastoral care of women –
another area we must consider in depth.

Innumerable tasks exist in the church –
complementary to rule and teaching – which
women ought to do and are not doing at present.
This needs to be explored in terms of the possible
implications of those who may be described as
'deaconesses' in 1 Timothy 3:11. We must define
the complementary nature of male and female
functions in the church (this we will also try to
do later).

Many problems we face in society stem from
the putting aside of the traditional, and often
biblical, roles of men and women, and their
mutual relationship. The Church of Jesus Christ
is charged to be different from the world – to
be as salt and light. Our contemporary society
has lost its way in understanding the proper
differences and complementary nature of men
and women. On the one hand women may be
debased as they are considered merely sex

objects or at best second-class citizens, or on the other hand there may be the pretence that equality means that men and women are basically the same in their functions in society, and in all their gifts.

Part of the Church's worldliness is that all too often she too has lost her way in this fundamental sphere of human relationships, although, in different ways. On the one hand she has so underlined male dominance that women have been relegated to insignificant functions in the Church and their gifts stifled. Or, on the other hand, the Church has been so swayed by the extremes of the feminist movement that she has acted as if there were no divinely intended differences in the functions of the sexes.

The Church should demonstrate the beauty and attractiveness of the complementary nature of male and female, even as Christians should in their marriages. The Church should show the world what the ideal relationship between the sexes should be. We should not behave as those who ask, 'What is permissible?' but those who act in the light of the answer to the far better question, 'What is beneficial and constructive?'

If women choose to assume the leadership role where it is neither appropriate nor necessary, they may be in danger of perpetuating Eve's original mistake. Such a suggestion may be regarded as anti-feminist, but it needs to be made in all honesty.

If we question the principles of Scripture where they are plainly stated, we need to have Paul's question addressed to us, 'Did the word of God originate with you? Or are you the only people it has reached?' (1 Cor 14:36).

Questions for discussion

1. Male and female are obviously different physically and biologically. In what other ways do they tend to be clearly different?

2. I have tried to draw a distinction between rules and principles. Provide illustrations from the Bible of both.

Chapter Five

Trying to Get Service and Ministry into Perspective

One of the snares of the present debate about women's place in the church is that ministry is so often thought of in terms of status. It is considered wrong, therefore, that women should be denied certain leadership roles and positions of authority because the implication of such concepts of status is that women are regarded as inferior.

A paradox of Christian leadership

If rule and authority in the church, together with the teaching function, are matters of status then clearly that inference is correct. But one of the paradoxes of Christian leadership is that it is *not* a matter of status.

What took the disciples' breath away was the manner in which our Lord Jesus Christ taught and demonstrated that status was not something they should covet and that they should deliberately avoid equating leadership with status. By washing their feet as their leader he sought to correct their erroneous concepts of leadership and authority (Jn

13:12–17). Real leadership is leadership by example.

Leadership does inevitably carry an element of authority, but authority is not a matter of status in the body of Christ. Significantly, in his list of gifts in Romans 12 (ie v 8) Paul does not place it at the top of the list.

Sadly, the Church – influenced by the standards and patterns of contemporary society – has in the past, and does now at times, equate leadership with status. That is certainly not a Christian attitude, and is a way of looking at things which needs to be rejected. It is part of the Church's worldliness.

A key concept

The concept of the body in 1 Corinthians 12 reminds us that the members of the body of Christ do not all have the same task or function. Not all *men*, for example, are called to teach or to rule. This in no way implies their inferiority to those who do. If secretly we think that it does, then we are misunderstanding the mind and will of our Lord Jesus Christ, the Head of the body, which is his Church. In the same way, women are not inferior because their particular task in the church is not to rule or to teach men.

Although women's tasks in some instances are different from those of men, their tasks are equally necessary and important to the body's well-being. No part of the body has status beyond any other part, except the Head, our

Lord Jesus Christ. He views each part of the body as equally important – whether male or female. It is he who, by his Spirit, determines the respective functions of each member.

The objection of some to the 'restrictions' upon women – that is to say, that they are not permitted to rule or teach men – is that this makes women seem less important than men. While not wanting to concede that this is so, because I personally do not regard women's ministry as unimportant in any respect, the biblical concept of the body has something important to say at this point.

Without identifying or naming those parts of the body which we may be inclined to call or regard as unimportant, we are told that such parts are often in fact the most important: 'Those parts of the body that seem to be weaker are indispensable' (1 Cor 12:22).

The peril of worldly thinking

If we are preoccupied with status, then we are worldly in our thought-patterns. We should put aside such thinking. This is relevant to us if we are leaders. We are not to lord it over others or to consider ourselves more important than those whom we lead. We are to see ourselves and prove ourselves to be the servants of those whom we lead.

Whether we are male or female, if we are in non-leadership functions, we should not be envious of those who are in such positions, and we are certainly not to feel ourselves inferior. Rather we are to see our functions as complementary – *because they are.*

What matters is not how the world at large sees our task or even how the body of Christ as a whole views it, but whether or not it is the task the Head has assigned us. To follow Paul's argument through, how stupid for an arm to try to be a foot, or vice versa. Equally stupid is it for a male to try to perform exclusively female functions in the body of Christ. The foot is not inferior to the arm, nor is the arm inferior to the foot. The female functions within the body of Christ are not inferior to the male, or vice versa. We need one another.

This concept of the body is the pre-eminent teaching in the New Testament when service and ministry are under discussion, and it must influence and dominate our thinking therefore when we consider women's ministry and service.

I admit that the world at large – with its abandonment of biblical authority and lack of a sense of God (the two are virtually synonymous) and its misunderstanding of the complementary nature of male and female – often sees women as unimportant in the life and leadership of the church. But according to 1 Corinthians 12 (and especially verse 22) the functions of those who appear 'unimportant' may be the most necessary and important if only we could see things as they really are. This is not written in a condescending manner as a kind of sop to women.

Ever since I first studied 1 Corinthians 12 in order to expound it, I have tried to come to terms with the fact that although as a pastor and teacher I appear prominent in the church, on the Day of Judgement I will discover that there are many other members of the church fellowships to which I have belonged whose contribution, although less conspicuous – and perhaps even hidden – will prove to have been as vital, or more so, than mine to the well-being of the body of Christ.

We do well to put the concept of the body (as expressed in 1 Corinthians 12, Romans 12:1–8 and 1 Peter 4:7–11) to the forefront of our discussion of women's ministry, recognising that different functions do not mean inequality or inferiority but rather mutual dependence and true equality and complementarity.

Ministry equals service

Unfortunately many parts of the Christian Church have fallen into the snare of regarding ministry as different from service. I confess to having been guilty of this myself in that from my conversion I was brought up to think of 'the ministry' – particularly of a pastor and minister of the gospel – as being something quite apart from other forms of Christian service. To go into the ministry was to become a pastor or 'minister'.

It is easy to see how this situation arose. It probably goes back to the early days of the Church when the apostles, aware that they could not fulfil their primary task of being pastors and teachers and at the same time care for the administration of relief for the poor and similar functions, instituted what we traditionally call the first 'deacons'. Their reasoning was, 'It would not be right for us to neglect *the ministry of the word of God* in order to wait on tables' (Acts 6:2, italics mine). This word 'ministry' is used on a number of occasions in the New Testament.

Because the references are principally in relation to our Lord's ministry and to that of the apostles – although not exclusively so (cf Col 4:17) – we have tended to associate 'ministry' with something special, like apostleship or, subsequently, holding an office in the church.

But the word itself simply means service (*diakonia*), a word found thirty-four times in the New Testament, often used to describe the most ordinary service, such as service at tables (Lk 10:40; Acts 6:2, etc), as well as other forms of service within the fellowship of God's people (1 Cor 16:15; Rev 2:19).

Our contemporary concept of ministry is not biblical if we limit ministry simply to pastors and leaders, and those who hold offices in the church such as elders or deacons, or by whatever other names church leaders are described. All Christians – male and female – are to be equipped and prepared 'for works of service [*diakonia*], so that the body of Christ may be built up' (Eph 4:12).

Those of us who are – to use the common phrase – 'in the ministry', are to teach and exemplify the truth that all Christians are called to minister, and that our own task is not to be exaggerated in its importance or to be seen as one conveying status.

If right concepts of service (ministry) are to be developed, those who give the whole of their time to teaching and preaching, and shepherding God's people, must see as one of their primary aims the development of spiritual gifts and forms of service in the life of *every* member of the body of Christ – both male *and* female (see Eph 4:11–13).

An observable danger

In our concern to get our calling to service and ministry right, we may lose sight of our principal calling – our calling to holiness and to witness (1 Cor 1:2; 1 Pet 1:15–16; 2:9–10). Both a Christian man's and a Christian woman's principal calling is to be holy because God himself is holy, and then to bear witness to his grace to them in Christ.

The life we live is far more important than the gifts we possess and the functions we fulfil in service in the church. What counts with God is not our function but our character. God's concern is not with our status but with our sanctity. Unless we hold on to basic truths like this, we may fail to see the wood for the trees in our debate concerning the place of women's ministry in the church.

Questions for discussion

1. How influenced in the church are we by worldly concepts of status? If we are, how do we go about correcting this mistake?

2. How did our Lord Jesus Christ exemplify that leadership is principally a matter of example?

Chapter Six

The Ordination of Women

It is the issue of the ordination of women that
has sparked off the current debate concerning
women's ministry in many parts of the Church.
Women's ordination has been the main public
issue because the ecumenical consequences have
captured the media's attention. Large
denominations such as the Anglican or Episcopal
Church are acutely aware that the ordination of
women will distance them from closer
relationships with the Roman Catholic Church,
and ecumenically they are committed to that
closer relationship.

The ordination of women to the priesthood
and hence to the episcopate presents an
insuperable barrier to the hoped-for restoration
of full communion with Rome. Nevertheless, the
Church of England seems set upon accepting
women's equal ordination with men to the
ministry. Many now consider it to be simply a
matter of time.

Other denominations have been ordaining
women to the ministry of the church for a
number of years. The Church of Scotland has
done so since 1970, having made women eligible
in 1968, and the United Free Church even earlier
in 1930. The Methodist Church in Britain first

ordained women in 1973 and the Congregational churches in 1917 (and in 1956 the first woman chaired their union of churches). Hence women ministers are found in the United Reformed Church – the consequence of the coming together of many Congregational and Presbyterian churches, especially in England. The Baptists in England and Wales ordain women. A woman minister's name was first added to the probationers' list in 1922 and to the full ministerial list in 1925. Women are not yet admitted to the ministerial list in Scotland, but a Report submitted to the Baptist Union of Scotland, entitled *Women in the Ministry*, proposed the acceptance of women as candidates for the ministry, but it did not receive the required majority in 1983.

The situation is not dissimilar worldwide, in smaller church bodies as well as larger. In 1988, for instance, the General Assembly of the Association of Churches of Christ in Nicaragua approved the resolution, 'Women as well as men can be appointed by the Church of Christ to occupy the position of pastor, teacher, theologian and other ministries exercised by the Church as well as leadership positions in the Church.' In July 1991 the Dutch Reformed Church in Africa decided that women may serve in the offices of pastor and elder.

People approach the question of ordination from many different angles. There is one particular angle from which I feel I must distance myself because of a basic doctrinal difference. Some argue against the ordination of women because they are against women *priests* and the views they hold concerning the service of Holy Communion or the Lord's Supper as a Mass.

We may sometimes discover ourselves arguing for the same practice as others but with totally different motives and convictions. I find myself in sympathy with a high churchman, for example, when he argues biblically for the non-ordination of women. However, I do not find myself in sympathy with some of the underlying grounds and motivation for his argument when he assumes that the Lord's Supper represents some kind of sacrifice at which men alone, who are ordained priests, may officiate.

A key question, therefore, is, 'What is ordination?' Is it ordination to priesthood or to the ministry of pastoring and teaching God's people? The New Testament finds no place for the former, but underlines the truth of the latter.

Ordination in the New Testament is always of elders (Acts 14:23; Tit 1:5). The New Testament knows nothing of what is commonly known as an 'apostolic succession'. Individuals were set apart for special ministry by the laying on of the hands of those in local leadership (Acts 13:1–3).

The principal 'ordination' or setting apart of individuals was to eldership. This gives a proper perspective, hopefully, to those of us who serve as pastors and teachers or 'ministers', in that we are simply elders – elders, who in terms of 1 Timothy 5:17, not only help 'direct the affairs of the church' but whose work also is 'preaching and teaching'.

A pastor and teacher – properly understood in terms of New Testament teaching and practice – is an elder among elders. He may be first among equals, if his fellow-elders choose to regard him as such, but pastors and teachers remain elders, and their ordination – if such takes place – is no different and no more significant than that of those elders whose principal task is to direct the affairs of the church, and who may not give the whole of their working time to it.

I favour the ordination of all elders where their appointment is seen as the deliberate recognition of the God-given gift of eldership. Public ordination has value only where it recognises what God has already done in the special calling of his Spirit and in the conferring of gifts of ministry. We cannot make 'ministers' or 'elders'; only God the Holy Spirit can do that. More crucial than human ordination is the Spirit's prior ordination or choice.

Much more important, therefore, than the question of the ordination of women is the question of whether or not women should be appointed as elders in the church – or deacons if a church has only deacons, since sometimes where a differentiation is not made between the two functions of elders and deacons, the same individuals tend to be expected to fulfil both tasks. Both elders and deacons must be spiritual people, but the primary responsibility of the elders is pastoral and that of the deacons is administrative.

Should women be elders? Should women be

elders whose public task is to rule and teach the whole congregation of God's people? If we allow ourselves to be conditioned by the contemporary trend to remove all distinctions and differences between men and women, we will be inclined to think that equality between the sexes demands that they should. But it is not a matter of equality, but rather God's establishment of the complementarity of the sexes' contribution to everyday life, as well as within the church.

While I would not want to place too much emphasis upon it, we cannot ignore our Lord's precedent in the choice of twelve *men* to be his apostles. Many women accompanied him in his ministry and were committed to his cause (Mk 15:40–41). But none of them was called to apostleship. Few, if any, would suggest that our Lord was influenced by tradition or the culture of the first century – and not least in his attitude to women. His attitude proved to be a liberating factor for them.

That being so, it does not seem unreasonable to ask, 'Why did not our Lord choose some women to be among his apostles if women's teaching and leadership ministry is intended to be the norm?'

A principle of Christian doctrine is the sufficiency of Scripture. Basic to that principle is the understanding that God – who is infinite in wisdom and knowledge – anticipated in his provision of the Scriptures all the situations with which his people would be faced in every age. With such an important issue as women's ministry as 'pastors and teachers', it is not unreasonable to argue that if such constitutes God's purpose there would be a clear statement to that effect.

The assumption in the New Testament, especially in the qualifications given for overseers (1 Tim 3:1–15) and elders (Tit 1:5–9), is that they should be men. This makes complete sense in that according to the New Testament and 1 Timothy 5:17 in particular, elders' tasks are to 'direct the affairs of the church well' (ie rule) and to preach and teach – the two tasks which we have seen from the New Testament are the responsibility of men, where such have the calling from God the Holy Spirit.

I always feel cautious about arguing from church history, because the Scriptures alone are our rule. But church history is not to be ignored, and is particularly helpful when it confirms that our understanding of the Scriptures is consistent with that of the Church over the centuries. The pattern of the early Church was not to have women elders (whether as 'pastors and teachers' or as those who shared in the direction of the churches' affairs). This pattern has continued throughout the centuries as the churches have been guided by the Scriptures and the Holy Spirit. I find it impossible to conceive of God keeping the Church in the dark for so long if he intended women's ministry to be the norm.

Some might argue that the Church has sometimes been blind and disobedient to God's will in the past – and in the present – as indeed it has and sadly often is. But in those periods when the Church has been revived by God's

Spirit and reformed by his Word, it has not led to any marked change of conviction concerning the proper relationship of men and women in the church so far as rule and teaching are concerned.

On the contrary it seems that it has sometimes been spiritual decline within the visible Church, and a lack of confidence in the authority and sufficiency of the Scriptures, together with the pressures of the feminist movement, that have produced some of the contemporary stimulus for change, rather than any discovery or rediscovery of God's truth.

It can be argued that in many cases the reason for the appointment of women to public ministry or as elders (or deacons) has been the shortage of men candidates.

Part of the Church's spiritual impotence has been its failure to reach men with the gospel. Many churches have a large preponderance of women. When a church constitution requires that it should have a set number of elders, it is understandable that the inclusion of women should be contemplated if no suitable men are available.

As a Church of Scotland minister said, 'If I have to choose between a man who has no spiritual life and who at best as an elder can knock a nail into a wall, and a converted woman who can pray, I have no hesitation in choosing the woman!' I can fully appreciate his pragmatic approach, although it is regrettable that circumstances should ever make the choice to be of that nature.

It ought to be said too that not all women by any means want women ministers or women elders (or deacons). It is impossible to know, of course, how many women would choose one rather than the other. Nor should the issue be resolved according to statistics for or against. Those who are most vocal in any discussion of the subject may not be any means represent the majority. Women who argue for women's ministry may suggest that women who do not do so are suffering from centuries of indoctrination. That may be true of some; but it cannot honestly be said of all. Some women feel unhappy about women's ministry in terms of rule and teaching because of their convictions from Scripture.

Down to practicalities

Key questions must be addressed. What should our relationship be to those churches and denominations which have already admitted women into their ordained ministry? What is to be our attitude to such women themselves, especially if we are pastors?

First and foremost, we must try to see this whole subject in perspective. The ordination of women, or the conviction that they should not be ordained, is not a fundamental of the gospel, or of the faith, and it should not therefore be elevated to such status. It is not worthy, therefore, of becoming a major cause of division between Christians and Christian churches.

There may sometimes be grounds for not having fellowship with other churches because of more basic questions which hide behind the issue of women priests and ministers. For example, if women's ministry is put forward by a church simply on the grounds of equality or expediency, and the Bible is regarded as irrelevant in what it says, any evangelical church will find little basis for fellowship with that church since it will have a diminished regard for the faith once for all delivered to God's people.

But if churches who genuinely hold to the authority of Scripture and to the faith decide that it is not inconsistent with such a position to call women as 'ministers' and as elders, then it is our Christian duty to accept those churches (Rom 15:7). We do not accept one another as Christians or as churches because we see eye to eye on everything, but rather because we recognise the grace of our Lord Jesus Christ in one another. We should accept such individuals and churches therefore with charity and courtesy.

Accepting one another, however, does not preclude the honesty which flows from love. In fact, it is when we *do* accept one another that we are able to be honest and open with each other, so that our understanding of God's truth is furthered. And such honesty is often lacking – and thus its helpful fruits – because we do not accept one another as we ought. Polarisation then takes place and frequently harms the body of Christ and spoils her testimony.

When we fail to communicate with those who are undoubtedly our brothers and sisters in Christ about things concerning which we differ, we do a disservice to our people because they are then put under pressure to conform to our position rather than to the Word of God looked at without prejudice. Our desire and determination must be to conform to God's Word and will, not to a position which we find comfortable.

Practical problems will have to be resolved if we adopt this attitude – an attitude which I believe to be right – towards churches which accept women as pastors, teachers and elders. A practical dilemma was shared with me recently by a church I visited. For decades they have joined together with several other evangelical churches for special Easter services. One of these churches has now called a woman minister. What should they do when the turn comes for this new minister to preach at the united service, especially if the church venue is a church which is unhappy at women's ordination to the ministry?

There will be endless permutations of such problematic circumstances to cope with, but it seems to me that certain principles should be applied to this example, and to other similar situations. First, we must be honest and courteous in expressing to the minister and church concerned any reservations we have. If they themselves are at all sensitive, they will anticipate that there may be problems, and will probably prefer that they should be brought out into the open. Simply to side-step the problem by manufacturing excuses for not participating as previously is sub-Christian behaviour.

Second, the decision about participation or non-participation must not be made personally if we are the pastor and teacher. It must be the decision of the church leadership.

Third, I must recognise that responsible as I may be for the discipline of the church fellowship to which I belong, I am not responsible for another church fellowship's pattern of church life and discipline. They – as we – must answer to the Lord, and I am not to be so presumptuous as to make judgements where God does not call me to do so.

Fourth, I must always remember that our fellowship is not simply with the minister of another church, or its corporate leadership, but with God's people who constitute that local church. We must be careful not to offend or hurt another part of the body of Christ.

Fifth, if we do decide to invite the female pastor and teacher to speak at the united service in our church, we should explain to our own church fellowship beforehand in a closed church meeting why we have done so, so that they realise that we have not changed our convictions, and that we are endeavouring not to elevate women's ministry to the position of a fundamental doctrine or a cause of disunity.

Sixth, if we decide that we would be creating a stumbling-block to some of our own church fellowship by asking or allowing the woman minister of the other church to preach in our church, the acceptable compromise would be to join together, but for the minister of the church where the joint meeting is held to be the speaker. Then the members of the other churches can decide for themselves – by their feet – what they wish to do.

Seventh, if it is felt that the whole issue of women's ministry will be either divisive or a stumbling-block to many within our church fellowship, and that it would be foolish to proceed, then the position should be honestly and graciously explained to the other church, possibly with the desire expressed to have fellowship together in other ways.

Whatever the different permutations of practical problems that arise we must aim at reacting positively rather than negatively where differences are not with regard to fundamental truths of the gospel. To maintain the unity of the Spirit in the bond of peace may often be costly and uncomfortable, but the Head of the Church makes it mandatory.

Questions for discussion

1. What place, if any, does ordination have in our church fellowship or group of churches to which we belong? Does it have the right place and is its significance understood?

2. How important an issue is women's ordination in our church fellowship? What are the principles underlying our church's position?

Chapter Seven

The Role of Women in Pastoral Care

The pastoral care of women should be the
particular responsibility of women, and not men
(eg Tit 2:3–5). As a general principle, it is both
ideal and advisable if women exercise pastoral
care for women, and men for men. If we follow
this guiding principle, we avoid many snares
which unhelpful emotional involvement with
someone of the opposite sex may bring – a
danger inherent in all close relationships
between the sexes.

This principle of the pastoral care of women
as the main responsibility of women may seem
to contradict the emphasis placed earlier upon
the New Testament's assumption that eldership
and the office of pastor and teacher should be
exercised by the male. I believe that there is no
conflict.

A distinction

A distinction needs to be made between pastoral
rule and pastoral *care*. Pastoral rule must
involve church discipline where such is
necessary, and that is the responsibility of the
elders, or whoever else fulfils a similar role in
the leadership of the church. Pastoral care,

however, which is the outflow of the primary gift of the Spirit – love – may be exercised, and ought to be exercised, by both men and women who are so gifted.

An example

What does this mean in practice? It is difficult to be practical without thinking of an actual situation, although each tends to be somewhat unique. The obvious thing for me to do is to describe the church setting with which I am most familiar, and apply what I think is right to it, in the hope that others will then be able to bring to bear the same principles on their own but different (and sometimes vastly different) local church context.

In the church of which I was latterly pastor for eighteen years, the leadership of the church was entrusted to the elders and the deacons. Being quite a large church by British standards, there were twenty elders and eighteen deacons. The elders met on their own at least once a month, and they gave themselves primarily to the determining of spiritual policy for the fellowship, and attention to spiritual needs that were brought to their notice. They then met with the deacons and, in theory at least, functioned as deacons rather than as elders, with the emphasis being upon administration, whether of finance or buildings. (I mention the deacons' meeting because in the next chapter I want to discuss the possibility of women deacons.)

The pastoral team – when at its full complement – was the senior pastor, an associate pastor, a young assistant pastor and a lady-worker or deaconess. The latter in turn had a team of women who assisted her in the visiting of women within the congregation because of the large number involved, especially of older women confined to their homes on account of illness or old age.

Weaknesses and remedies

There are weaknesses in this arrangement, in spite of the fact that it worked well. The weaknesses arise from an absence of a clear structure of communication between the groups involved in pastoral care. The weaknesses can be overcome by careful spiritual administration on the part of the pastor or his associate; but if those individuals are not there or are not alert, there can be a breakdown of communication between the elders and the pastoral team, and the elders and the women visitors.

In such a situation, we need to ensure first that women – and, of course, men too – are properly cared for spiritually. We also need to equip a group of women to fulfil this essential task for women.

In this church situation I have described, the elders rightly had overall responsibility for the spiritual well-being of the church fellowship, each of the twenty elders had special responsibility for his pastoral group (approximately one-twentieth of the membership). However, it was inappropriate for them to exercise pastoral care personally when it necessitated visiting young single girls in their homes, or older married or single women, apart from the elderly.

Although ideally perhaps the elders' wives ought to be able to assist their husbands, not all are able or qualified to do so. The fact that wives are spiritually one with their husbands and fully supportive of them does not immediately qualify them or obligate them to be involved in extensive pastoral care. Family commitments, for example, may make that impossible.

The way forward

The way forward is to recognise the proper distinction between pastoral rule (the responsibility of the elders) and pastoral care (the responsibility of those gifted for it, and those delegated this task by the church).

If, therefore, we think of a church fellowship divided into pastoral groups, with an elder responsible for each, I would see the elder continuing to be answerable for the pastoral care of all the members of his group. He, and sometimes, where appropriate, with his wife, would concentrate on the pastoral care of families, elderly men and women and single men. Then either his wife or a spiritually sensitive and able woman would endeavour to care for the other women within the group.

Their responsibility would not simply be to visit the unwell and the elderly, but to identify the lonely, others with special needs, and those not yet effectively integrated into the life of the church fellowship, so as to get alongside them, where possible, in order to encourage them. An elder and his wife may enlist the help of a small 'team' to help them. Besides lightening their load, it also serves to train and discover future elders.

A women's pastoral team

How would this work? I envisage a strengthening of the team of women who regularly visit women linked with the congregation. In a church with a lady-worker or deaconess, they would work alongside her, and, ideally, under her leadership. I would encourage them to meet together two or three times a year for the sharing of spiritual needs, for a review of their work, and for prayer.

If suitable people are not available, a church should not appoint a fixed number of women as pastoral carers simply to satisfy some arbitrary target. The qualifications for such women ought to be established, just as they are in the New Testament for elders. Above all they should be spiritual women, who have a good reputation both within and outside the fellowship, and who are marked by discretion.

Just as the elders would regularly review the spiritual well-being of the members of their groups as necessary, in the course of their elders' meetings, so the women pastoral carers would meet to do the same thing, and with the purpose of encouraging one another too in what can sometimes be a discouraging task.

The women's pastoral team's meeting would need someone of sensitivity with leadership qualities to chair it, and to guide its proceedings. If a church has a deaconess or lady-worker in the pastoral team, she would normally be the ideal person to do this. If not, either the elders could nominate or appoint a suitable person, or let the women themselves nominate one of their members, subject to the elders' agreement.

Lines of communication are vital in pastoral care, especially where responsibility is delegated. The pastor or his deputy should sit in on the regular meetings of the women pastoral carers from time to time, so as to identify with them, to encourage them, and to ensure that the women have the ear of the elders in any concerns they express.

Along with this, if the person who chairs the women carers' meeting is not a deaconess or lady-worker, I would want to invite that person to meet the elders two or three times a year, in order to give encouragement to that person in her leadership and to share more intimately in needs for prayer which could not be shared in a larger and more public meeting. If in a larger church there is a regular staff meeting, then that might be an alternative.

Action required

Two important courses of action are necessary if women are to be encouraged to take their proper place in pastoral care.

First, the church must be educated to expect women to exercise pastoral concern for their own sex. Speaking generally, while men expect pastoral care from men, women do not expect it from women. This is a fruit of our over-emphasis upon male ministry.

We ought to be quite open about the reasons for our wanting the sexes to care for members of their own sex. We live in a world where many of the wise barriers and courtesies between the sexes have been removed – sometimes with disastrous results. This has overflowed into the church, and ministries and lives have been ruined because careful discretion has not been exercised, and barriers against over-involvement ignored. The name of our Lord Jesus Christ has then been dishonoured, and members of his flock caused to stumble because men and women have refused to recognise their vulnerability.

Second, we must provide training in pastoral care – both for men and for women. I would not want to over-emphasise training because I recognise that spiritual qualities and wisdom are the priorities, but we all benefit from instruction from those who have more experience than ourselves. We have perhaps forgotten that basic to pastoral care is the giving of counsel from the Scriptures, and applying their principles to every area of daily life. Pastoral care is essentially a Bible-teaching role. If women are to exercise pastoral care for women, they need to be as biblically well-taught as men who exercise the same function for men. I fear that we sadly fail to do this more often than not for those men called to be elders in our church fellowships.

Ideally, the pastor should share with his fellow elders and women pastoral carers his own experience and convictions about the basic principles of pastoral care and practice. This could be done initially when the church pastoral committee is set up, and then perhaps recorded on tape so that new additions to the team may gain from it too.

I would also recommend that on those occasions when the pastor sits in on the meeting of the women pastoral carers he should discuss a different spiritual need or problem and how to relate to it – ie helping the backslider, the new Christian, the bereaved, etc. It is important not to take small things for granted like the ideal length of a hospital visit, and the obvious times to avoid calling on people in their homes.

Recognition

The women's team of pastoral carers should be recognised by the church just as the elders or spiritual leaders of the church are recognised within the church fellowship. When first instituted, it would be worthwhile considering having a service of commissioning, or better still to include such within the context of a Sunday service when the majority of the church membership will be present. This commissioning should be accompanied by an exposition of Scripture concerning the exercise of pastoral care and the duty of all Christians to recognise their need of it.

Untapped resources

It is to our shame that considerable untapped resources of pastoral care by women in the churches have not been utilised and developed. There are insights and sensitivities women possess that are special to them, and which are invaluable to the well-being of the body of Christ.

Whatever our church situation, we need the pastoral gifts – and the administrative gifts – or women. We must see them released. That will require change, initiative, organisation and determination. Providing we see the difference between rule and care, and teach and demonstrate the difference, no reasonable objections to women's ministry can be raised. In fact, we will wonder why we did not see its place and priority before.

Questions for discussion

1. How effectively do we feel our church fellowship exercises pastoral care? What are its strengths and its weaknesses?

2. If we are already involved in pastoral care, what are the most important lessons our experience has taught us?

3. If we are not involved in pastoral care, but are perhaps called to it in the future, in what areas would we most feel in need of instruction?

Chapter Eight

The Role of Women in Administration or as Deacons/Deaconesses

Since women have a vital place in pastoral care – as we have demonstrated – they certainly have a place in spiritual administration. This raises the question of whether or not there should be women deacons or deaconesses. The issue is complicated by confusion of language in that we use the same names in our churches and denominations to describe different offices and functions.

In some non-conformist churches there are both elders and deacons. A few have just elders. In far more, there are only deacons, and the deacons – or some of them – perform in effect the duties of elders. In Anglicanism or Episcopalianism a deacon ranks just below a priest.

Guided by the New Testament, we will think of elders or pastors as those set aside for the spiritual direction, rule, care and teaching of God's people. Deacons are those to whom specific tasks of service are assigned, as in the case of Stephen and his colleagues in Acts 6, irrespective of whether or not these men were officially described at the time as deacons, since we do not know.

If it is clearly and unequivocally established that the resonsibility for rule and public teaching of the whole congregation rests with the elders, and not with the deacons, I see no reason why women should not be deacons or deaconesses, although I have wondered why in Acts 6 the apostles were so specific in requiring that the 'brothers' should 'choose seven men' to accept what we would regard as deacons' responsibilities. But such a question cannot be answered because the seven men appointed were not called deacons, much as their task was to serve.

The word 'deacon' itself implies the absence of rule and focuses instead upon straightforward serving. If the deacons do indeed 'rule' – ie exercise discipline over the church, etc – then women should not be appointed as deacons. But where deaconship is exercised in parallel with eldership, then there is no bar to women becoming deacons or deaconesses.

Sadly, because of a failure so often to differentiate between the separate functions of elders and deacons, we have lost both the contribution of women to pastoral care and their equally important contribution to the spiritual administration of the church's life, which is so fundamental to its well-being.

Once again, it is necessary for me to apply my convictions to the specific situation with which I am familiar, in the hope that others will be able to apply the same principles to theirs.

Where there are both elders and deacons, the

ideal is for the number of deacons to be indefinite or flexible, so that the body of deacons is made up of those who have come to the fore because of the specific tasks they already fulfil for the benefit of the whole church fellowship.

There is an important difference between the elders' and deacons' tasks. *All* elders are called to 'rule' and exercise corporate pastoral care of the congregation, although not all will be called to teach and preach in public. The deacons, however, will tend to have various tasks, some closely associated, but different nevertheless. Tasks and functions will be wisely delegated so that too heavy a load of administration does not rest upon any one individual.

The ideal procedure will be that any person who is unproved or untried in a task should be initially asked to do it without being invited to become a deacon. Once he or she has proved himself or herself, he or she should then be invited to become a deacon by the other deacons. Deaconship would then last as long as the particular office was held or the specific function fulfilled.

The advantage of such a procedure is that there is no 'dead wood' among the deacons. In other words, there are no members who are deacons in name only. Each will have a specific task to perform for the benefit of the church. Each will have a contribution to make to the matters under discussion from the viewpoint of the area of responsibility held.

The day-to-day administrative work of the local church is best done by smaller committees of the deacons rather than by all the deacons meeting together. These committees should meet more frequently than the general deacons' meeting. Obvious committees would be those dealing with finance, missionary responsibilities, catering, editorial work (including the church magazine), the church fabric and buildings and – in our case – the running of an old people's home. Each committee should have a person to chair it, and that person ought to be a deacon.

Within such deacons' committees, both men and women should be members, chosen not on account of their sex but according to their gifts and the contribution they can make.

When the deacons come together under such an arrangement, they will either be those who chair a committee or those who have specific responsibilities for definable and practical tasks, such as stewarding, publicity, etc.

In the situation with which I am familiar, the church treasurer is an elder. He certainly does not need to be an elder, and he could just as well be a deacon, and perhaps more appropriately so. On account of his responsibilities of eldership, most of his treasurership functions are delegated to deacons, with one looking after covenants, another salaries, and yet another attending to day-to-day expenditure. The treasurer's brief is to co-ordinate these activities, and to keep the elders in touch with the financial state of the church, which can have its own spiritual significance, for finance is not just a matter of administration.

Any one of these delegated financial

responsibilities could be exercised by a woman or by a man. All assistant treasurers within the church should be considered as potential deacons or deaconesses while they perform such tasks.

The responsibility for church catering and hospitality in all its various forms usually falls to a woman. Such a person, once proved, should be considered as a potential deacon or deaconess, and then function as such all the time these responsibilities continue to be exercised.

A church magazine is an important vehicle for communication within a church fellowship. The editor of this may often be female. As editor she too should be considered as a possible deacon or deaconess.

Any pastor knows that there are all kinds of practical emergencies which arise within a fellowship where love and care are priorities. A practical action group needs to leap into action immediately such crises present themselves. Here women come into their own. Women are unique in the practical care they are able to exercise. It is no accident that women are outstanding in all the caring professions, such as nursing. Paul lists some of the activities that mark godly women – 'showing hospitality, washing the feet of the saints, helping those in trouble and devoting [themselves] to all kinds of good deeds' (1 Tim 5:10). Men may and must also exercise such practical care, but they are not as good or as competent at it as are women.

With deacons each representing areas of responsibility within the church, the main function of the deacons' meeting would be effective communication between the different areas of the church's work, a sharing by the elders of convictions they have for the church's progress in obedience to God, and dealing with practical issues and recommendations from the deacons' committees. The elders would need to determine whether or not they should all be present at deacons' meetings or, instead, represented, perhaps in rotation, by a proportion of their number. I personally prefer a full attendance, so as not to separate the elders and deacons from fellowship together, provided the meetings are not frequent and burdensome. Each church needs to determine the most appropriate procedure.

In cases where there is only one leadership group – say only deacons – it is not as easy to achieve the rightful inclusion of women's ministry. But it can be done. Usually there will be a variety of committees which handle aspects of the church's life. Women should be invited on to these committees, just as men are, according to the gifts that are needed, and the contribution they can make. But to have a clear demarcation between the functions of elders and deacons is an important key to success.

An ideal arrangement

The ideal structures, in the situation with which I am familiar, therefore, would be something after the following pattern. First, there would be the elders, all men, with each having pastoral responsibility for a proportion of the membership. With them would rest the responsibility of spiritual discipline and policy, and of safeguarding and encouraging the ministry of the Word.

Second, there would be a women's pastoral group, which would meet regularly several times a year. On occasions the pastor and the pastoral team would attend, as suggested, so that pastoral concerns could be shared, and spiritual priorities determined. On such occasions elders should feel free to attend, but it should not be expected of them. Realism dictates that we should not overload ourselves with attendance at meetings where our involvement is not essential.

Third, there would be the deacons, both male and female, with each deacon having a specific task. The basic purpose of the deacons' meeting would be the co-ordination of all the different aspects of the church's life, especially administratively, and to provide a forum and platform for the elders to share convictions prior to sharing them with the whole church fellowship. At such meetings the elders as a whole or their representatives would 'fly a kite' when they had new ideas and convictions, and the various committees would do likewise.

The deacons' function would not be rule – ie to exercise spiritual discipline – or to organise teaching. These responsibilities would clearly rest with the elders. Basic to a deacon's function would be either the chairmanship of a committee or the fulfilling of a defined task. All committees would be made up of men and women with a contribution to make.

Inevitably more men than women may be on some committees than others, and vice versa. But that is a matter of indifference providing both are eligible for inclusion, and membership is based upon gift rather than sex.

Committees ought to have clearly defined responsibilities and powers, so that they can act in those areas for which they have responsibility, and yet at the same time be called to answer for their decisions when all the deacons meet. Committees should meet more frequently than the whole company of deacons together.

The elders – either as a whole or by delegated representatives – should always meet with the deacons in their general meeting in order to cultivate a close sense of identity, and so that if any subject arises which might be considered a matter for rule or teaching, they may establish that to be the case, and immediately transfer it to the elders' agenda for action.

An important part of the deacons' coming together with the elders should be for prayer, not as a secondary purpose, but as a primary.

I am not suggesting that the implementing of structures like this or those similar will be easy, but I believe it to be necessary. We tend to go to extremes – either denying women their place altogether or totally ignoring the principle that rule and teaching are assigned by God to the male eldership, or their equivalent. We must aim at balance – not the balance of accommodation, or compromise, or trying to please everyone. But the balance of Scripture, recognising that male and female *are* complementary, and that their different functions are to be recognised and rejoiced in, and not considered as being in competition or rivalry.

Questions for discussion

1. Do our church structure make it easy for the complementarity of male and female functions to be expressed? Are there practical steps that can be taken to improve this expression?

2. In what spheres – generally speaking – do we feel that women are more able administratively, and in what areas are men more able?

3. How would you meet the objection to women's involvement as deacons or deaconesses, voiced perhaps in the comment, 'It's the thin edge of the wedge – deacons today, but elders tomorrow'?

Chapter Nine

Women as Teachers

Rule and teaching are two parallel functions of spiritual leadership. Guided by the New Testament, it is plain that as a general principle women should not teach men in a local church context. Both 1 Corinthians 14:34–35 and 1 Timothy 2:11–12 indicate that a woman's function is not that of a teacher in church services where men and women meet together for worship and instruction.

It needs to be said here, as elsewhere, that this is a general principle to be applied consistently, but always with care and spiritual sensitivity. It does not rule out the spiritual leaders of a church – ie the elders or their equivalent – inviting a woman to teach or preach in what we may describe as 'one off' situations. For example, a woman may have particular experience and insight into the care of those who have been bereaved of their marriage partner. She might well be invited to share her insights with the whole church fellowship.

Sadly, here as elsewhere, we have gone to extremes. If we believe that the responsibility for the ministry of the Word within church services is with men, we have tended then to overlook altogether women's teaching gifts. This is to our shame and to the church's great loss. Numerous opportunities exist for teaching and preaching in women's meetings, young wives' groups, women's evangelistic supper clubs, and the like. The teaching potential of such is frequently neglected and underrated.

Spheres of teaching

Writing as a pastor, while my Sunday ministry has always been a first priority, much of my teaching has been on a one-to-one basis and also in small groups, especially discipleship classes or classes for new Christians.

Just as women should exercise pastoral care for women, so women should teach women, complementing the public teaching given by pastors and teachers in meetings of the church. To the forefront should be one-to-one teaching. Nothing can surpass the value of personal discipling of new Christians. But plainly this is never something that a man should do for a woman, or a woman for a man.

Having already instructed older men in their duties, Paul instructs older women 'to teach what is good' (Tit 2:3). 'They can train the younger women to love their husbands and children, to be self-controlled and pure, to be busy at home, to be kind, and to be subject to their husbands, so that no one will malign the word of God' (Tit 2:4–5). Paul uses the two important verbs 'to teach' and 'to train'.

Seldom, however, do we encourage and train

women to teach and to train others in this way. That needs to be done, even as it needs to be done for men. Women also need to be sensitive to the gifts of those women within the church fellowship from whom they should profit in this way. Women sometimes look to men for instruction when in fact that instruction may come equally well – or better – from a member of their own sex.

We tend to denigrate today in society the most important sphere of all for teaching – the home. Mothers are to instruct their children in Christian truth. Bringing up children is the responsibility of both parents (Deut 6:4–9; Eph 6:4; 1 Tim 5:10; cf 2 Tim 1:5; 3:15) but where the husband is the wage-earner, the greater burden tends to fall upon the wife and mother. The example of a mother's and a grandmother's faith may be a key factor in the development of a child's faith (2 Tim 1:5). We often fail to give instruction to parents in the ways in which they should teach their children the faith. Women have a pre-eminent place in this – and they are to be honoured for it.

Discipleship classes or new Christians' groups

Classes for the instruction and discipling of new Christians go under a variety of names in the churches. Women should be encouraged and trained to disciple women, both on a one-to-one basis and in groups.

Where a group of new Christians – male and female – are instructed together, it is good for there to be both a male and a female leader of the group, and for them to share the teaching, with the possibility of them sometimes separating into the two groups according to sex to consider the implications of some Christian truth from a male and female viewpoint.

The encouragement of teaching gifts

Few churches will encourage and develop teaching gifts within their membership without establishing some kind of teaching and preaching classes on a regular if infrequent basis. These classes should be conducted by those who regularly minister to the church fellowship so that the importance of the classes is clearly established. They should be open to both men and women. Individuals with known gifts should be encouraged to attend by the spiritual leadership of the church.

The existence of such classes also provides an opportunity for those with yet undiscovered or hidden gifts to identify themselves, and for their gifts to be unearthed. Instruction should be given about teaching and preaching, and examples provided of how to go about preparing an address or talk. At the same time, up to two members of the class should be given the opportunity to speak for, say, twelve minutes, having a prayer meeting or the giving of an epilogue as their imagined context. Then the class should assess their contribution and make constructive comments on both material and presentation. I listened to four people do this recently in a preaching class at a Bible college. In this instance, the two women did better than the two men! Instruction should also be given in how to use the Bible in groups and in one-to-one pastoral and teaching situations.

We have sought to apply the teaching of the New Testament that as a general *principle* men should have the responsibility for public teaching, for that seems to be the straight-forward implication of its teaching. A principle of this nature is not to be applied with the rigorousness of a law. A principle is not to be applied so strictly and legalistically that it contradicts other equally valid principles.* Where men are not available, women may then teach. In other words, the principle that God's people need to be fed by those called to do so is more important than the identity of those who feed God's flock. Principles need to be applied in harmony with each other.

Public ministry of the Word is the task of the male elder or teaching elder. One-to-one teaching is the task of male and female to their own sex. Public ministry to women in their different groups ought to be much more with women than it is, and training should be given to foster and develop teaching gifts.

The gifts and abilities so encouraged, developed and exercised may be called upon on occasions by the whole church, perhaps sometimes for public ministry – not as the norm but as the exception, where the church leadership recognises its appropriateness.

Questions for discussion

1. How should we expect to recognise that an individual has a teaching gift?
2. What qualities would we expect to accompany the teaching gift if it is to be used in the church?

Chapter Ten

A Proper Objective

The debate concerning women's ministry is bound to continue. People will come to the subject with a variety of motives and preconceptions. We cannot help doing so ourselves.

The issue will never be resolved to everyone's satisfaction. Sadly, some do not accept the Scriptures as relevant at all in the debate. Even those who accept the authority of Scripture may differ in their interpretation of crucial scriptures. The more we explore the scholarly exegesis of the key passages, the less inclined we are to be dogmatic about their precise interpretation where there are uncertainties.

What then is the way forward? Do we simply despair? Do we conclude that it is something every person must decide for himself or herself? I do not think so because this is a church or corporate matter rather than merely a matter of personal preference. Unless we grapple with this issue Christians are going to be divided, not only within denominations but within individual church fellowships.

The way forward is to establish what we should be aiming at, and the principles we should be unashamed of holding on to, and yet always with humility and charity. The spirit in which discussions on this subject take place is almost as crucial as the subject itself.

Our objective

Our objective should be to ensure that the church – and in particular our own local Church fellowship – is the sphere in which the true complementarity of men and women is displayed.

The world at large does not see this complementarity, but it needs to do so. Men and women are not the same in their gifts – just as they are not the same in their physiology and temperamental make-up. This is true both within and outside the Church.

Men and women possess by nature a delightful complementarity, and the Church, as God's redeemed people, should display this in a unique way. Restored to God, we are restored to some degree at least to what God wants us to be, and to how he originally created us to function. God purposed the sexes to be complementary, and not in rivalry. He intended men and women to have different functions and gifts, and to respect each other's unique qualities.

The local church should strive to recognise the gifts of its female members as much as those of its male members. Although the gifts of rule and teaching have been foremost in our discussion, and are clearly prominent in any list of the Lord Jesus Christ's gifts to his people, they are not his only gifts to them for their common good.

This must be seen and taught from the Scriptures.

The local church – and its leadership in particular – must review its structures and life, and honestly ask itself, 'Are we utilising the gifts of our women members as much as those of our men?' That question should be regularly on their agenda until the principle is plainly worked out, and not least in women teaching women and caring pastorally for them. A necessary practical step in some situations will be the establishment of an eldership in distinction to deaconship so that women may be admitted to the latter.

But there are other fronts where the church must not be inactive. Part of the church's honouring of marriage (Heb 13:4) is the high place it should give to the harmonious relationship of husband and wife, and their majoring on gladly fulfilling their responsibilities to one another. A husband is to care for his wife and to see his principal function as working in order to provide for her and any family they may have. It may seem old-fashioned, but it is God's unchanging will and purpose. A wife's first duty is to be a 'helper suitable' for her husband (Gen 2:18).

The Church must uphold the dignity not only of marriage but of motherhood. The contemporary view of a woman as either a wife or mother is summed up in the attitude which says of such, if she has no other employment, 'She is *only* a housewife.' The world would tend to pour scorn on the Book of Proverbs' description of a wife of noble character (Prov

31:10–31). But to uphold such ideals is a vital part of the Church's contribution to the well-being of contemporary society as salt and light.

The woman who decides to stay at home and to abandon her former career or daily work is not second rate or a non-achiever. A wife and mother should major on home-making – and do so without apology. We lose something of infinite value to society if we denigrate the primary responsibility a mother has for caring for her children. This is not to suggest that it is wrong for a wife and mother to go out to work, or, on occasions because of necessity, to exchange roles with her husband, providing they are agreed that it is in the best interests of the family. Husbands need to be encouraged to realise that their role within the home is as important as any roles they may exercise outside of it (eg 1 Tim 3:4–5).

In marriage preparation we have perhaps failed to establish these principles, so that couples find themselves moulded by the world's values and attitudes rather than by God's Word. This then overflows into the church. The fact that Paul urged godly women to 'train the younger women to love their husbands and children' (Tit 2:4) is a reminder that the basics should not be taken for granted.

No one could pretend that all is well with family life in the western world when such a large proportion of marriages break up in divorce and where child abuse affects every strata of society. We have nothing to be ashamed of in standing by the Bible's teaching concerning the family, and the world at large needs the crucial influence of this teaching. If Christians do not give it, who will? That teaching cannot be separated from recognising the complementarity of men and women, and the unique contribution women have as mothers to the well-being and instruction of their children.

Acknowledging that there is much work to be done, we must avoid allowing women's ministry to become the major issue and getting it out of perspective. To some, that may seem to be mere male chauvinism on my part. But my concern is pastoral. As a pastor I always avoided talking about difficulties in the church in front of my children while they were growing up because I did not want them to have a jaundiced view of the Christian Church. Similarly, I believe mothers should be careful how they talk about these issues in front of their children as they may unconsciously impart a restrictive view of the Church which becomes a stumbling-block.

A final plea

While women's ministry is an important issue for any church fellowship to come to agreement about, it ought to be decided even before discussion takes place that no one will allow it to divide the church fellowship. As the Report of the Study Panel of the Free Church of Scotland (1989) suggests, 'The issue threatens to be every bit as divisive as the charismatic controversy.'

The subject is important, but it is not important enough to divide the body of Christ. It does not appear in any doctrinal basis or credal statement, and it is not to be elevated to that place of importance.

We must aim at discussing it with a desire to understand what God says to us in his Word. We must put off as best we can the spectacles of male chauvinism or extreme feminism. Where the Scriptures are clear, we must be clear. Where the Scriptures are unclear or silent, we must respect the views and interpretations of others.

Rather than being guided by our personal interpretations of scriptures which are unclear and subject to unresolved debate, we must be guided by those general scriptural principles which are indisputably clear. This determination will be challenging to implement. It will mean choosing what is beneficial rather than what is permissible, seeking the good of others rather than our own good (1 Cor 10:23–24), and making every effort to keep the unity of the Spirit through the bond of peace (Eph 4:3). Where our honest and united desire is to honour our Lord Jesus and to discern his will, we will find the right way forward, and the church will be built up rather than divided. With nothing less dare we be satisfied.

Questions for discussion

1. What should we be aiming at with regard to more effective women's ministry in our church fellowship?

2. How can we ensure that any discussion of the subject does not become divisive?